The Garden, the Ark, the Tower, the Temple

Cover Illustration
The Garden of Eden, with Adam and Eve on either side of the tree of knowledge, around which the serpent coils as it places the fruit of the tree into Eve's hand. Surrounding the scene is a variety of animals, including fabulous beasts, that co-existed together without fear of one another or of man in a state of paradise. From catalogue no. 1, plate detail.

The Garden, the Ark, the Tower, the Temple

Biblical Metaphors of Knowledge in Early Modern Europe

Jim Bennett and Scott Mandelbrote

Museum of the History of Science in association with the Bodleian Library

Published in the United Kingdom by the
Museum of the History of Science, Broad Street, Oxford,
in association with the Bodleian Library, Oxford.

First published in April, 1998
© 1998, Jim Bennett and Scott Mandelbrote (text)
© 1998, Museum of the History of Science (figures 20 and 43)
© 1998, Bodleian Library (remaining figures)

A CIP record for this book is available from the British Library.
Cataloguing note: there is no 'and' in the title of this book, real or implied.

ISBN 0-903364-09-3

All rights reserved.
No part of this publication may be stored, reproduced, or transmitted,
in any form or by any means, electronic, mechanical, or otherwise,
without the prior permission of the publisher.

The publication of this catalogue was made possible by the support of
the Foundation for Intellectual History.

Thanks to: Ashmolean Museum, Edward Adcock, Norma Aubertin-Potter, Paola Bertucci, Constance Blackwell, Reg Carr, Nick Cistone, Koenraad Van Cleempoel, Codrington Library, Joanna Dodsworth, Sam Eidenow, Clare Griffiths, William Hodges, Clive Hurst, Stephen Johnston, Dana Josephson, Dot Little, Giles Mandelbrote, Ilaria Meliconi, Jackie Merralls, Simon Pulleyn, University Museum of Natural History, Charles Webster, Frances Willmoth.

Ark and Temple sections, descriptions of portraits, instruments, and other objects are written by Jim Bennett; Bibles, Hartlib, Garden, Tower, Hartlib Circle and Biblical Criticism sections by Scott Mandelbrote; Introduction jointly.

Catalogue design, typesetting and figure captioning by Giles Hudson
Photography: Bodleian Library Photographic Studio and Giles Hudson
Image adjustment by Suzy Brown

Set in Monotype Garamond and Garamond Antiqua
Printed in Oxford by Fine Print (Services) Limited

An electronic edition of this catalogue, which includes a full-text
search facility, may be found on the Internet at http://www.mhs.ox.ac.uk/

Published to accompany the exhibition of the same name held in the
Bodleian Library Exhibitions Room, 2nd February to 2nd May, 1998.

CONTENTS

7	Introduction	
13	Bibles	catalogue nos. 1–8
33	Samuel Hartlib	catalogue nos. 9–12
43	The Garden	catalogue nos. 13–26
73	The Ark	catalogue nos. 27–38
103	The Tower	catalogue nos. 39–50
135	The Temple	catalogue nos. 51–60
157	Hartlib Circle	catalogue nos. 61–68
169	Biblical Criticism	catalogue nos. 69–86

Figure 1
'And when the woman saw, that the tree *was*
good for food, and that it *was* pleasant to the eyes, and a
tree to be desired to make *one* wise, she took of the fruit thereof,
and did eat, and gave also unto her husband with her, and he did eat.'
Genesis 3: 6. From catalogue no. 1, plate detail.

INTRODUCTION

The stories of the Garden of Eden, Noah's Ark, the Tower of Babel, and the Temple of Solomon are among the best known in the Old Testament. They were alluded to frequently during the sixteenth and seventeenth centuries, and were often used at that time to frame accounts of the progress of knowledge. The narrative history which could be found in the Bible presented a coherent story of the growth and decline of knowledge, in which moral and spiritual factors helped to determine natural and practical outcomes.

As metaphors of knowledge, the four stories gave information about both the acquisition and the ideal state of human understanding. But they also issued warnings about the necessary difference between human and divine knowledge and suggested ways by which knowledge might be married to piety and wisdom in order to achieve an improvement in the condition of mankind. The image that they conjured up was thus both hopeful and threatening. It demanded that human beings temper material and intellectual change with spiritual or moral development. The stories seemed to many to allow for the possibility of transforming the world through the application of human intellect and endeavour. Yet they also emphasized the contemporary belief that the earth had once been a better place, and that human ignorance and suffering were themselves the products of disobedience, error, and folly. The knowledge which was needed to change human life and the natural environment for the good depended on

Introduction

an understanding of the dangers of moral frailty as well as of the achievements of intellectual ingenuity. That understanding could best be developed through an awareness of biblical history and a sense of the working of providence, both of which were enhanced by acquaintance with the lessons of the Garden, the Ark, the Tower, and the Temple.

The Garden of Eden provided the setting for the Fall, a transformation which brought about the loss of both spiritual and intellectual perfection, corrupting the nature of humans and of the surrounding environment. The Garden symbolized the ideal state, when the earth had been spontaneously fertile, labour was easy and fulfilling, and human activity had been grounded on a complete knowledge of both words and things. A return to this paradise was considered by some in the sixteenth and seventeenth centuries to be possible through the restoration of learning, and through striving to bring the earth and its inhabitants back to a pristine state of grace. It could also be achieved by practical measures, such as the establishment of botanical gardens, which reunited the plants of the world in a single space, or the planting of fruit trees, whose cultivation mimicked the dutiful dressing of the Garden of Eden by its first inhabitants, Adam and Eve. By the zealous investigation of nature and the searching out of new varieties of plants and techniques of husbandry, the world might be rescued from corruption and infertility. Hard labour could make the Garden grow again, and restore the knowledge which humans had once employed to govern nature in paradise.

The hopeful message of the Garden was reinforced by the story of the Flood and of Noah's Ark, which told how God had restored humanity's dominion over the earth, and how he had preserved the innocent parts of his creation from the destruction which punished the corrupt. The Ark also seemed to provide a pattern for a number of actions that might help to recreate human power over nature, lost initially at the Fall. It was an inspiration to collect animals and natural objects, and then to classify them as a step towards the recreation of true knowledge. Applied as a metaphor, the Ark allowed contemporary collectors to become Noahs. Their collections came to represent new Arks, in which learning could be expanded and completed. The knowledge which might be amassed in these modern Arks was to be part of an encyclopaedic compendium of nature. Ordered by the application of reformed philosophical principles, it would mirror and rival the comprehensive understanding of the natural world once possessed by Adam or by Noah. The achievement of this end required the establishment of new techniques and practices of learning and teaching as well as the building of new institutions and collections. Inspired by the story of the Ark, many early modern authors and collectors saw themselves as rescuing human knowledge and understanding of the natural world from neglect and depravity.

But the story of the Ark was accompanied in the Bible by a warning, in the shape of the story of the Tower of Babel. Here, human pride had again led to the loss of control over nature, through the confusion of language with which God had frustrated the overweening ambition of the Tower's builders. The knowledge of the just was humble as well as pure; its achievement depended on the ability of people to overcome the limitations of their fallen state, notably the divisions of language and of race which frustrated real communication. The task of overturning the curse of Babel was one to which early modern scholars therefore had to turn themselves.

The mechanism used by God to bring about the dispersion of peoples after Babel had been the multiplication of languages. The study of languages, their relationships and their distribution was thus a tool for discovering how the earth had been peopled after the Flood. It stimulated both linguistic and ethnographic knowledge, and also encouraged the investigation of the natural world. Adam's language, the first tongue spoken by mankind, had been perfectly adapted to understanding the natural world and all the species of things which it contained. It was thought to have survived in a corrupted form until the building of Babel. Although the original, ideal speech of humanity was now lost, its essence could be recovered through the construction of a 'philosophical' language. This would restore the direct linkage between words and things, recreating many of the characteristics of Adam's language. Its grammar would reflect natural relationships unambiguously and would open up the possibility of universal communication once again. The groundwork for the construction of new philosophical languages consisted of the analysis of natural history and the establishment of a profound natural philosophy, based on the species and operations which could be discovered by direct study of the natural world. It combined the endeavours of collecting, experimenting, ordering, and naming which fascinated early modern students of nature and which had once been the occupations of both Adam and Noah themselves. The attempt to reverse the curse of Babel became a means to return mankind to a pristine state of grace and knowledge whose defining characteristics were the complete understanding of philosophy and of the natural world and a renewal of unity between nations through shared language and mutual comprehension.

The negative aspects of the image of the Tower were in turn balanced by the positive vision of the Temple, a building which embodied God's purpose for his people, and which testified to the holy achievement of knowledge correctly applied. The architectural accomplishment of the Temple was understood to have been outstanding, while its inspired design embodied the principles of a divine geometry whose recovery would be a brilliant achievement for practical mathematics. The establishment of a convincing historical case for Solomon's use of a particular architectural style would confer on it an irrefutable legitimacy. Biblical accounts of the Temple demonstrated the significance which God had attached to standards of measure and their importance for the proper regulation of society. The ancient Jewish measures were embodied in the dimensions of

Introduction

the sacred objects of the Temple whose management was entrusted to the holy offices of the priests. Christian scholars of the sixteenth and seventeenth centuries felt that it was important to trace the descent of standards of measure and to recover their original values. Just as the recreation of some form of universal language might help to restore the knowledge of the world which had once been enjoyed by Adam and Noah, so the adoption of true universal measures might re-establish human dominion over the form and use of nature. The biblical account of the ancient cubit provided a model for the ideal standard of measurement which encouraged critics to believe that an equivalent universal measure might be based on a natural standard that could be used by men everywhere.

The extraordinary success of Solomon's mathematical ventures pointed to his profound natural knowledge and spiritual virtue. The wisdom which Solomon displayed, and which became his proverbial attribute, could only have been achieved through application, study and systematic work since he lived long after the Fall and the loss by humanity of its original, pure understanding of things. Solomon, and the house which he constructed for God, thus became models for the advancement and application of knowledge through organized, collective effort that inspired the creation of new institutions dedicated to natural philosophical learning and experimentation. As metaphors, they summed up contemporary aspirations to understand and control the natural world, and as historical exemplars they testified to the possibility that such hopes might actually be realized.

The ideas of the humanists and reformers of the sixteenth century encouraged early modern readers of the Bible to interpret the Old Testament as literal history, not as allegory. This led early modern writers about natural knowledge to turn to the stories of the Garden and of the Tower to explain the present state of mankind. It allowed them to see the project of overturning the Fall, and recreating the Ark or the Temple, as an essential part of humanity's return to grace and understanding. The stories of the Old Testament were not just convenient metaphors, let alone fictions, they were facts which taught by example how human beings ought and ought not to behave in order to attain knowledge. Although they were commonplaces of early modern learned writing, the Garden, the Ark, the Tower, and the Temple were especially prominent images in the ideas of a loose circle of authors, projectors, and thinkers which formed in England around the émigré German activist, Samuel Hartlib, from the 1630s to the 1660s. A great deal is known about the work of Samuel Hartlib and his associates during this period of great political, religious, and intellectual upheaval, because of the energetic publishing schemes which they pursued, and because of the survival of most of Hartlib's extensive correspondence.

Introduction

Letters and books by Hartlib and his friends demonstrate the central place which biblical themes had in their thought. Works on agriculture focused on plans to restore the pristine fertility of the earth through improvements in husbandry, and on the application of new techniques to the creation of beautiful gardens in seventeenth-century Oxford and elsewhere. The botanical knowledge collected in such gardens helped to inspire plans for new arks of learning in contemporary ideas about museums and places for scientific endeavour. The restoration of knowledge which could be achieved in these institutions is exemplified by discoveries made with new scientific instruments, such as the telescope or the microscope, which promised to restore the sensory perfection enjoyed by Adam in the Garden of Eden. The work of classifying nature carried out in botanic gardens and museums was extended in contemporary plans, sponsored by members of the Hartlib circle, for a universal language which would overcome the effects of Babel, and embody in their new names the rediscovered essences of things. Books dealing with the Tower emphasize this linguistic project, as well as the historical understanding of the role of Babel in promoting the dispersion of peoples, and the creation of modern nations. The hopes for a restoration of religion and worship, following on from the rediscovery of true knowledge, are displayed in contemporary plans of the Temple of Jerusalem, and in schemes for its rebuilding.

The works represented in this catalogue provide a view of the activities of the Hartlib circle, as part of a broader picture of the role of biblical interpretation in early modern Europe. They show how stories from the Bible provided coherent explanations for the human condition, and how they also seemed to offer plans for escape into a better world. The inspiration provided by the historical examples found in the Bible may seem strange or foreign to some modern readers. Yet it is surely essential to understand such unfamiliar things in order to make sense of past efforts to investigate and control the natural world. Only by doing so can we begin to unpick our own stories of the development of scientific practice, which have often rested on the achievements and discoveries of the seventeenth century.

Cataloguing conventions

In addition to the author, title and standard bibliographical details for each book, collation details, dimensions of the text block, and the Bodleian Library shelfmark of the edition described are also given. Collation descriptions follow Philip Gaskell, *A New Introduction to Bibliography* (Oxford, 1972). References in the text cited 'Hartlib Papers' are to: Judith Crawford *et al.* (eds.), *The Hartlib Papers: A Complete Text and Image Database of the Papers of Samuel Hartlib (c. 1600–1662) Held in Sheffield University Library* (2 CD-ROMs, Ann Arbor, Michigan: UMI Research Publications, 1995, ISBN 0835723682).

Figure 2
A page from Brian Walton's *Biblia sacra polyglotta*, the
London Polyglot, published in six volumes from 1653 to 1657.
Catalogue no. 73, p. 8.

BIBLES

During the sixteenth and seventeenth centuries, there was an increasing demand for vernacular translations of the Bible. This was stimulated by the writings and teachings of humanists and reformers, and sustained by the doctrines and liturgies of the new Protestant churches. Reformed church services assumed the provision of copies of the scriptures in the vernacular, so that the text of the set lessons could be read aloud to the people. Individuals purchased copies of the Bible in a wide variety of styles and sizes, for reading aloud to their families at home, for private study, or as pocket books which could accompany them to sermons and lectures. In several countries, political and ecclesiastical authorities sought to control the theological consequences of the demand for the scriptures by sponsoring official, national translations. One of these was the Authorized Version of the English Bible, produced by committees of learned translators, and first published in 1611.

Over the course of the seventeenth century, editions of the Authorized Version eventually displaced alternative English translations, such as the Geneva version (catalogue no. 4), from the market. The longevity and success of the Authorized Version was not inevitable. During the 1650s especially, its critics mounted a series of attempts to have the English translation altered or replaced. Some wished to see it provided with additional notes, to aid interpretation by the individual reader; others wished to amend the text or even translate it again from the original languages.

Although the Authorized Version was confirmed as the standard English translation of the Bible after the restoration of the monarchy and the Church of England in 1660, the arguments used by its critics were not entirely the product of radical or sectarian discomfort with an official text. Much of the language of the Authorized Version was drawn directly from the first published English Bibles, translated in the 1520s and 1530s by William Tyndale. A good deal of this seemed archaic or even incomprehensible to readers and hearers of the mid-seventeenth century. Furthermore, there were places where the Authorized Version mistranslated passages or where scholarly advances made the choice of words seem ill-judged. It was also a fact that the Authorized Version was shaped to the doctrinal assumptions of the Church of England, which were heavily criticized during the period of the Civil Wars and Interregnum in the 1640s and 1650s. There was, then, an argument for the revision of the Authorized Version, which appealed, for example, to some of Samuel Hartlib's friends. However, at the Restoration, that case was generally rejected as showing contempt for authority.

Despite its popularity, the Bible remained an expensive book for much of the seventeenth century. In part, this was because it was a large work, which required the use of a lot of paper – normally the most expensive component of the early modern book. Its production was complicated by the theological demand that its text be printed to a very high level of accuracy, in order not to mislead readers who had been taught that their religion was founded on the literal interpretation of scripture. This requirement was often used as an excuse to defend the monopoly of the King's Printers over the publication of the Bible, in particular the Authorized Version. Although it was not unusual for the right to publish steady-selling books to be vested as a monopoly in the hands of small groups of booksellers and printers, each holding a share in the copy, in the case of the Bible the practice did generate occasional controversy. Objections were raised against profiteering and it was sometimes argued that competition would improve the quality of printing, as well as lowering the price of the book. In the late 1620s and 1630s, the University of Cambridge embarrassed the King's Printers by exercising its right to print folio Bibles and by the high quality of its work (see catalogue no. 3).

However, real attempts to break into the King's Printers' monopoly, by producing rival editions of smaller format Bibles, only became possible with the breakdown of the authority of the Crown and of the Stationers' Company during the 1640s. Then a number of printers brought out alternative editions of the Authorized Version, and prices fell dramatically. Unfortunately, quality was often sacrificed, and worries also surfaced about the increasing spread of pirated editions of the Bible, especially those imported from Holland. Following the Restoration, the King's Printers came to arrangements with some of their rivals and were largely successful in reasserting their rights, although they had to fight off a serious challenge from the Oxford University Press in the 1670s and 1680s. Despite the survival of the monopoly, Bibles did become more affordable than they had been in the 1630s, in part because of a trend towards the production of smaller books printed on poorer paper. At the end of the seventeenth century, when wages were also higher, a standard, octavo edition of the Bible might have cost four shillings (unbound), compared with a price of more than six shillings in the 1630s.

The Bibles represented here range from the very grand to the relatively humble. The Bible was an essential part of the personal property of devout men and women, and individual copies often reflected the taste, wealth, and piety of their owners. These factors often shaped the choice of format, which could also be affected by the use to which the owner intended to put the book. They certainly determined the binding of the Bible (catalogue no. 8, for example), which was frequently a much greater expense than the purchase of the book itself.

Most of the Bibles described here could be illustrated with separately-purchased engravings. Several London printsellers stocked series of cuts for binding up with Bibles, and such pictures were intended to bring out the narrative elements of scripture in much the same way as the chapter headings printed in the text. They were clearly objects of delight as well as of instruction, and seem to have been particularly popular with wealthy female readers, and perhaps also with the purchasers of Bibles intended as gifts for children. Their presence in copies of the Bible was, however, exceptional. In the middle years of the seventeenth century, most people would have read the plain text of scripture, and, for reasons of theology, would probably not have wanted anything more. Children were brought up to read the historical narratives of the Old Testament first of all, perhaps initially picking up the thread from the chapter headings. This inculcated a sense of the Bible as exemplary story and as historical truth which never left most people.

Bibles

1. *The Holy Bible ... Illustrated wth Chorographical Sculps. by J. Ogilby*
    2 vols, Cambridge, 1660
    vol. 1: fol. in 4s: π² ¶-2¶⁴ A-2L⁴ (Genesis to Job)
    374 × 214 mm
    Bib. Eng. 1660 b. 1

In 1660, John Ogilby (1600-76) reissued the large folio Bible of 1659, published by John Field, the printer to the University of Cambridge, with a number of additional engraved plates that he had selected. Field's Bible was sponsored by Samuel Hartlib's friend, John Worthington, whilst he was vice-chancellor, in order to ensure the supply of a well-printed edition of the Bible for use in churches or libraries. Worthington told Hartlib that 'For a fair large letter, large paper, with fair margin, &c., there was never such a Bible in being' (*Diary and Correspondence*, vol. 1, p. 119). Most of the edition was, however, bought up by Ogilby.

The plate which is displayed here was engraved by Pierre Lombart and illustrates the story to be found in Genesis, chapters 2 and 3, although it is usually bound before the opening of the Old Testament at Genesis 1. It shows the Garden of Eden, with Adam and Eve on either side of the tree of knowledge, around which the serpent coils as it places a fruit from the tree into Eve's right hand. Surrounding this scene are the various animals and birds which inhabited the Garden: peacocks, pheasants, monkeys and squirrels populate the branches of the tree; birds fill the skies around it, and on the ground a wide variety of animals co-exist without fear of one another or of the man and the woman. These animals include fabulous beasts, such as the unicorn.

Ogilby had a varied career, originally as a dancing master, but later as a director of plays, a translator, a poet, and, most importantly, a bookseller and publisher. Until his stock was consumed by the Great Fire of London, in 1666, Ogilby specialized in the publication of illustrated works. He had been particularly impressed by the production of the London Polyglot Bible (catalogue no. 73), and especially by the plates engraved for it by Wenceslaus Hollar. As a counterpart to the Polyglot, he planned an edition of the Bible in all the major modern European languages (which was never undertaken), and a fine folio English Bible, which, in the end, was produced in time to be presented to Charles II on his first coming to the Royal Chapel at Whitehall in 1660.

For this issue, Ogilby supplied eight whole sheet engravings, seven of which were by Hollar, and had been intended as illustrations to the Polyglot, and one of which was by Lombart. Ogilby illustrated most copies of his Bible, however, with cuts bought from the Amsterdam publisher, Nicolaes Visscher (see cata-

Bibles

Figure 3
Engraved plate from Ogilby's 1660 Bible illustrating the state of paradise at the moment of the Fall. The plate was engraved by Pierre Lombart (1620?–1681). From catalogue no. 1.

18

logue no. 7). Visscher supplied Ogilby with sets of engravings from his own stock, most of which were the work of Cornelis Visscher, after Rubens, de Vos, de Bruyn, Tintoretto and others. Ogilby's ventures were successful in winning him royal favour, and, after the disaster of the Great Fire, he received a licence as a cosmographer and geographic printer, and embarked on the work of surveying Great Britain.

Ogilby's Bible was a very expensive book, and large paper copies of it may have cost as much as £25, even in sheets. It was not a financial success, however, and Ogilby failed in his attempt, in 1661, to have the publication of other illustrated Bibles prohibited for ten years. Though criticized later for inaccuracies in its printing, it presented the standard text of the Authorized Version in perhaps the most impressive form available in the mid-seventeenth century. Its illustrations were works of the best artists, and allowed those who could afford the book to visualize the events of the Bible in a grand style. Although Samuel Pepys complained, when offered a copy, that 'it is like to be so big; that I shall not use it, it being too great to stir up and down without much trouble, which I shall not like nor do intend it for' (*Diary*, vol. 7, p. 237–8), Ogilby's Bible found favour as a gift, for example accompanying Sir Richard Fanshawe on his embassy to Portugal in 1660. News of the printing of Field's edition of the Bible, and perhaps of Ogilby's plans for it, had excited Henry Oldenburg to write to Hartlib on the 2nd July 1659, asking after 'that gallant new Edition Bible printing at Cambridge' (*Hartlib Papers*, 39/3/28A-B).

T. H. Darlow and H. F. Moule, *Historical Catalogue of Printed Editions of the English Bible 1525–1961* (revised and expanded by A. S. Herbert, London, 1968), p. 206, nos. 666 & 668; T. S. R. Boase, 'Macklin and Bowyer', *Journal of the Warburg and Courtauld Institutes*, vol. 26 (1963), pp. 148–77; David McKitterick, *A History of Cambridge University Press: Volume 1: Printing and the Book Trade in Cambridge, 1534–1698* (Cambridge, 1992), pp. 327–8; Margaret Schuchard, *John Ogilby, 1600–1676* (Hamburg, 1973); Margaret Schuchard, *A Descriptive Bibliography of the Works of John Ogilby and William Morgan* (Frankfurt, 1975); James Crossley (ed.), *The Diary and Correspondence of Dr. John Worthington* (2 vols. in 3 parts, Manchester, 1847–86, Chetham Society, vols. 13, 36 & 114), vol. 1, pp. 119, 191, 192, 352 & 355; *Calendar of State Papers Domestic* (1661-2), pp. 67–8; Robert Latham and William Matthews (eds.), *The Diary of Samuel Pepys* (11 vols, London, 1970–83), vol. 7, pp. 237–8; John Loftis (ed.), *The Memoirs of Anne, Lady Halkett and Ann, Lady Fanshawe* (Oxford, 1979), p. 143.

Bibles

Figure 4
John Ogilby (1600–76), one-time dance master, director of plays, translator, poet, and, most significantly, bookseller and publisher. As a publisher Ogilby specialized in illustrated works, including the handsome folio Bible of 1660. Catalogue no. 2.

2. Portrait of John Ogilby
   By Sir Peter Lely
   Oil on canvas
   750 × 610 mm
   Lane Poole no. 146

   Ogilby is represented by catalogue no. 1.

   R. Lane Poole, *Catalogue of Portraits in the Possession of the University, Colleges, City, and County of Oxford* (3 vols, Oxford, 1912–26), vol. 1, p. 59.

Bibles

Figure 5 (Right)
The 1638 Cambridge edition of the Bible, shown here open at the first page of the Old Testament, the start of the first creation narrative in Genesis. Catalogue no. 3, p. 1.

3. *The Holy Bible Containing the Old Testament and the New*
    Cambridge, 1638
    fol. in 6s: π^2 A-3G^6 3H-3I^4 3K-3X^6 3Y^4 (Old Testament and Apocrypha); A-R^6 (New Testament)
    330 × 210 mm
    Bib. Eng. 1638 b. 1

Printed by the University Printers, Thomas Buck and Roger Daniel, this edition of the Authorized Version was considered by many seventeenth-century commentators to be the best available at the time, and it largely escaped the criticisms levelled at contemporary editions of the Bible by mid-century reformers. This opinion of its pre-eminence was also shared by most later authors, and it remained the standard text of the Authorized Version until 1762. The edition of 1638 built on corrections introduced into the Cambridge Bible of 1629, and incorporated revisions by Samuel Ward, Thomas Goad, John Bois, and Joseph Mede (an early friend and correspondent of Hartlib).

Although John Worthington later came to prefer Field's Bible of 1659, he had informed Hartlib in 1653 that 'the best Bible that ever hath been printed, in England is that by Daniel in folio with great Letters, which is most exactly and correctly performed' (*Hartlib Papers*, 28/2/77A [*Ephemerides*, 1653]). Like others, he particularly valued those revisions which made it more accurate than contemporary editions produced by the King's Printers in London, and appreciated the exactness and clarity of its typography, especially its use of italics to denote words and clauses, necessary to the sense of the English translation, but not to be found in the original Hebrew or Greek. The 1638 Cambridge Bible was printed in three sizes, at prices ranging from sixteen shillings to thirty shillings, unbound.

T. H. Darlow and H. F. Moule, *Historical Catalogue of Printed Editions of the English Bible 1525–1961* (revised and expanded by A. S. Herbert, London, 1968), p. 176, no. 520; B. J. McMullin, 'The 1629 Cambridge Bible', *Transactions of the Cambridge Bibliographical Society*, vol. 8 (1981–4), pp. 381–97; David McKitterick, 'Customer, Reader and Bookbinder: Buying a Bible in 1630', *The Book Collector*, vol. 40 (1991), pp. 382–406.

¶ The first book of MOSES called
GENESIS.

CHAP. I.

1 *The creation of heaven and earth, 3 of the light, 6 of the firmament, 9 of the earth separated from the waters, 11 and made fruitfull, 14 of the sunne, moon, and starres, 20 of fish and fowl, 24 of beasts and cattel, 26 of man in the image of God. 29 Also the appointment of food.*

*Psal.33.6. and 136.5. Acts 14.15. and 17.24. Heb 11.3.

IN * the beginning God created the heaven and the earth.

2 And the earth was without form and void, and darknesse *was* upon the face of the deep: and the Spirit of God moved upon the face of the waters.

*2.Cor.4.6.

3 And God said, * Let there be light: and there was light.

4 And God saw the light, that *it was* good:

†Heb. between the light and between the darknesse.
†Heb. and the evening was, and the morning was, &c.
*Psal.136.5. Jerem. 10.12. and 51.15.
†Heb. expansion.

and God divided † the light from the darknesse.

5 And God called the light Day, and the darknesse he called Night: † and the evening and the morning were the first day.

6 ¶ And God said, * Let there be a † firmament in the midst of the waters, and let it divide the waters from the waters.

7 And God made the firmament, and divided the waters which *were* under the firmament, from the waters which *were* above the firmament: and it was so.

8 And God called the firmament Heaven: and the evening & the morning were the second day.

*Job.38.8. Psal.33.7. and 136.6.

9 ¶ And God said, * Let the waters under the heaven be gathered together unto one place, and let the drie-land appear: and it was so.

10 And God called the drie-land Earth, and the gathering together of the waters called he Seas: and God saw that *it was* good.

11 And God said, Let the earth bring forth † grasse, the herb yeelding seed, *and* the fruit-tree yeelding fruit after his kind, whose seed *is* in it self, upon the earth: and it was so.

†Heb. tender grasse.

12 And the earth brought forth grasse, *and* herb yeelding seed after his kind, and the tree yeelding fruit, whose seed *was* in it self, after his kind: and God saw that *it was* good.

13 And the evening and the morning were the third day.

*Deut.4.19. Psal.136.7.
†Heb. between the day and between the night.

14 ¶ And God said, Let there be * lights in the firmament of the heaven, to divide † the day from the night: and let them be for signes, and for seasons, and for dayes, and yeares.

15 And let them be for lights in the firmament of the heaven, to give light upon the earth: and it was so.

16 And God made two great lights; the greater light † to rule the day, and the lesser light to rule the night: *he made* the starres also.

†Heb. for the rule of the day, &c.

17 And God set them in the firmament of the heaven, to give light upon the earth,

18 And to * rule over the day and over the night, and to divide the light from the darknesse: and God saw that *it was* good.

*Jer.31.35.

19 And the evening and the morning were the fourth day.

20 And God said, * Let the waters bring forth abundantly the ||moving creature that hath † life, and fowl *that* may flie above the earth in the † open firmament of heaven.

*2.Esdr.6.47.
||Or, creeping.
†Heb. soul.
†Heb. face of the firmament of heaven.

21 And God created great whales, and every living creature that moveth, which the waters brought forth abundantly after their kind, and every winged fowl after his kind: and God saw that *it was* good.

22 And God blessed them, saying, * Be fruitfull, and multiply, and fill the waters in the seas, and let fowl multiply in the earth.

*Chap.8.17. and 9.1.

23 And the evening and the morning were the fifth day.

24 ¶ And God said, Let the earth bring forth the living creature after his kind, cattel and creeping thing and beast of the earth after his kind: and it was so.

25 And God made the beast of the earth after his kind, and cattel after their kind, and every thing that creepeth upon the earth after his kind: and God saw that *it was* good.

26 ¶ And God said, * Let us make man in our image, after our likenesse: and let them have dominion over the fish of the sea, and over the fowl of the aire, and over the cattel, and over all the earth, and over every creeping thing that creepeth upon the earth.

*Chap.5.1. Wisd.2.23. 1.Cor.11.7. Ephef.4.24. Col.3.10.

27 So God created man in his own image, in the image of God created he him: * male and female created he them.

*Matth.19.4.

28 And God blessed them, and God said unto them, * Be fruitfull, and multiply, and replenish the earth, and subdue it: and have dominion over the fish of the sea, and over the fowl of the aire, and over every living thing that † moveth upon the earth.

*Chap.9.1.
†Heb. creepeth

29 ¶ And God said, Behold, I have given you every herb † bearing seed, which *is* upon the face of all the earth, and every tree, in the which *is* the fruit of a tree yeelding seed: * to you it shall be for meat.

†Heb. seeding seed.
*Chap.9.3.

30 And to every beast of the earth, and to every fowl of the aire, and to every thing that creepeth upon the earth, wherein *there is* † life, I have given every green herb for meat: and it was so.

†Heb. a living soul.

31 And

Bibles

4. *The Bible*
London, 1615
4° in 8s: ¶⁴ A–2Q⁸ (Old Testament); 2R–2Z⁸ 2&⁸ 2∗⁴ (Apocrypha);
   3A–3Q⁸ 3R⁴ (New Testament and Tables)
198 × 136 mm
Bib. Eng. 1615 e. 1(2)

From the time of its first publication in 1560, the 'Geneva version' of the English translation of the Bible enjoyed widespread popularity. It provided a clear, readable setting of the text, in formats which were, at least relatively, affordable (this Bible probably cost about seven shillings, unbound). Moreover, it supplied a wide variety of interpretative aids to its readers, especially in some later recensions which incorporated the notes to the New Testament of Laurence Tomson (1539–1608). From 1599, Tomson's notes on the Book of Revelation were displaced by those of Franciscus Junius (1545–1602) in some editions. In addition to notes which clarified the sense of the text, and extensive cross-referencing, the Geneva Bible provided helpful tables, which gave order to scripture, and maps and diagrams which helped readers to picture the setting of biblical stories.

Much of the additional information to be found in the Geneva Bible derived from the scholarship of John Calvin and Theodore Beza, the leading figures of the first and second generations of the Reformation in Geneva itself, and the theological mentors of many reformed congregations across Europe during the second half of the sixteenth century, and thereafter. Thus, the map of the situation of Eden (displayed opposite), derived originally from an in-text map published in the 1553 French edition of Calvin's commentary on the Book of Genesis. A copy of the map had first appeared in Bibles published in Geneva in 1560, amongst which was the first edition of the 'Geneva version' of the English Bible, prepared by English Protestant exiles in the city. The presence of maps from Calvin's commentary on Genesis was one sign of the commitment of the editors of the Geneva Bible to a historical reading of the Bible. Maps which claimed to show the exact situation of places named in scripture seemed to prove that the Bible told a continuous story about the real world. They justified a literal reading of the text, by showing how it corresponded to presumed geographical facts.

However, the interpretative apparatus of the Geneva Bible proved controversial in the eyes of many readers, and criticisms were also made of the choices of words, in particular of ecclesiastical terms, made by the translators. Such criticism intensified in the years following the publication of the Authorized Version of 1611, whose clear text, with an apparatus limited to a selection of biblical cross-

Figure 6
Map of the situation of the Garden of Eden, from a London edition of the Geneva Bible. The inclusion in scripture of maps purporting to show the location of the places mentioned reinforced a literal reading of the text of the Bible and reflected the desire of editors to demonstrate that it related a true historical account of the world.
Catalogue no. 4, sig. A2.

references, deliberately sought to eschew controversy. After 1616, Robert Barker, whose family had held the right to print the Geneva Bible in England since the first English edition of 1575, ceased to reprint the whole Bible in the Geneva version, concentrating instead on the publication of the Authorized Version, to which, as one of the King's Printers, he also held the copyright. The existence of a continuing market for the Geneva Bible in England can, however, be inferred from a number of pirated editions, and from imports from Holland. Many of Hartlib's correspondents would certainly have been aware of the readings given in the Geneva Bible, and most of them subscribed to the historical and literal principles for reading scripture which it embodied.

T. H. Darlow and H. F. Moule, *Historical Catalogue of Printed Editions of the English Bible 1525–1961* (revised and expanded by A. S. Herbert, London, 1968), p. 143, no. 342; John David Alexander, 'The Genevan Version of the Bible: Its Origin, Translation, and Influence', unpublished D. Phil. thesis, University of Oxford, 1957; Irena Backus, 'Laurence Tomson (1539-1608) and Elizabethan Puritanism', *Journal of Ecclesiastical History*, vol. 28 (1977), pp. 17-27; Catherine Delano-Smith and Elizabeth Morley Ingram, *Maps in Bibles 1500–1600* (Geneva, 1991), pp. 4-7, & p. 19; Charles Eason, *The Genevan Bible: Notes on its Production and Distribution* (Dublin, 1937); Naseeb Shaheen, 'Misconceptions about the Geneva Bible', *Studies in Bibliography*, vol. 37 (1984), pp. 156-8; Maurice S. Betteridge, 'The Bitter Notes: The Geneva Bible and its Annotations', *Sixteenth Century Journal*, vol. 14 (1983), pp. 41-62.

Bibles

5. English Delftware Dish
   circa 1660–75
   406 mm in diameter
   Ashmolean Museum, Warren Collection of English Delft, no. 8

   A London-made polychrome dish depicting Adam and Eve with the tree and the serpent in the Garden of Eden.

   A. Ray, *English Delftware in the Robert Hall Warren Collection, Ashmolean Museum, Oxford* (London, 1968).

6. *A Compleat Collection of Cutts of the Old Testament*
   London, 1716
   8°: title-page and 98 numbered full page engravings
       bound with a similar collection of 100 New Testament cuts
   180 × 111 mm
   Opie L 59

   Although much later than most of the other books represented here, this volume of 'cuts' is representative of a style of biblical illustration dating back to the 1620s. Its opening four pages are unusual in having been coloured by hand, almost certainly by an early owner. The page displayed opposite depicts the Fall; it shows Eve on the point of handing to Adam the fruit of the tree of knowledge, which she has already taken from the serpent. As yet, the fruit is uneaten, since, according to many contemporary theologians, Adam was the first to sin. Animals recline in the foreground, and wander peacefully in the background. Beneath the picture, extracts from the relevant verses of the third chapter of Genesis have been engraved, and the whole page bears the title: 'Mans fall by the Serpents deceit. Gen. 3'.

   The history of this picture is complicated. In 1716, it was published as part of a discrete collection of biblical cuts, intended to help the young 'attain to the knowledge of the historical and most remarkable passages' of scripture. The pictures in this collection, however, are simply reversed copies of engravings which could have been bought, either separately, or as a set of illustrations for binding with a copy of the Bible, during the 1690s. The illustrations of the 1690s are themselves enlargements of cuts made by Frederick Henderick van Hove (*c.* 1628–1698), and first published in London in 1671. Almost all of van Hove's cuts derive their inspiration from the series of biblical pictures engraved

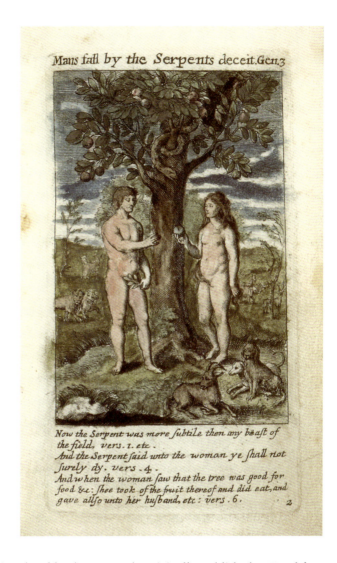

Figure 7
Hand-coloured engraving of the Fall, from a collection published in 1716. Eve is illustrated offering Adam the fruit of the tree of knowledge. This is depicted as yet uneaten, reflecting contemporary belief that Adam was the first to sin. Catalogue no. 6, plate 2.

by Matthaeus Merian the elder (1593–1650), originally published at Frankfurt from 1625 to 1627, and reissued at Strassburg in 1630. From the late 1640s, Merian's work was extensively copied by Dutch engravers (see catalogue no. 7), some of whose illustrations to the Bible circulated in England. Van Hove was the first of a number of artists working in England during the second half of the seventeenth century to base his biblical illustrations on Merian's engravings. His cut of the Fall is rather more loosely grounded on Merian's original than most of his other biblical pictures.

Apart from Merian's engravings, the most-widely available biblical illustrations in England during the 1640s and 1650s were those of Jacob Florensz van

Figure 8
Noah praying as the animals enter the Ark. Catalogue no. 6, plate 5.

Langeren, which were issued with dedicatory verses to Charles I by William Slatyer, treasurer of St David's (see catalogue no. 8). These cuts, which were based on pictures by Maerten de Vos, influenced later Dutch engravers, and may have inspired van Hove's depiction of the Creation. In general, illustrations of the Bible, which could be bound with the text, served to personalize books, and to encourage readers to assimilate the highpoints of scripture history. They tended to be expensive, however, and they were also theologically suspect in the eyes of many of the hotter sort of Protestants. Thus, the practice of binding pictures with the English text of the Bible was attacked as Popish and idolatrous at the trial of Archbishop Laud, and, again, by the bookseller Michael Sparke in the 1650s.

T. H. Darlow and H. F. Moule, *Historical Catalogue of Printed Editions of the English Bible 1525–1961* (revised and expanded by A. S. Herbert, London, 1968), p. 228, no. 824; T. S. R. Boase, 'Macklin and Bowyer', *Journal of the Warburg and Courtauld Institutes*, vol. 26 (1963), pp. 148-77; G. E. Bentley, jr., 'Images of the Word: Separately Published English Bible Illustrations 1539-1830', *Studies in Bibliography*, vol. 47 (1994), pp. 103-28; Lucas Heinrich Wüthrich, *Das druckgraphische Werk von Matthaeus Merian d. Ae.*, vol. 3 (Hamburg, 1993), pp. 1-58; Diane Kelsey McColley, *A Gust for Paradise: Milton's Eden and the Visual Arts* (Urbana and Chicago, 1993), pp. 72-4 and figs. 1-12; George Henderson, 'Bible Illustration in the Age of Laud', *Transactions of the Cambridge Bibliographical Society*, vol. 8 (1981-84), pp. 173-216; [Michael Sparke], *A Second Beacon Fired by Scintilla* (London, 1652). A complete set of the illustrations to Genesis by Slatyer and van Langeren can be found in the Bodleian Library at the shelfmark Vet. A2 f. 49.

7. Nicolaes Visscher
Figures of the Bible in Wich Almost Every History of the Holy Scriptures is Discribed
Amsterdam, no date
4°: A-2Y⁴ A-Y⁴
130 × 155 mm
Antiq. e. N. 11

From the late 1640s, collections of biblical illustrations based on Matthaeus Merian's engravings began to appear from Dutch publishers, in particular the Danckerts and the Visscher families. One of the most successful of these collections used the reworking of Merian's illustrations by Pieter Hendriksz Schut (1619–62), with accompanying poetic summaries of the biblical text (perhaps by Reinier Anslo), which were also translated into Latin, French, German and English. This copy, which is a finely-bound oblong quarto, was probably part of the first printing, executed for Nicolaes Visscher in around 1648. Illustrated (overleaf) is the seventh engraving, showing the situation of Adam and Eve after the Fall and their expulsion from paradise. In the background, Adam ploughs the land, which has grown less fertile as a result of God's curse upon it (Genesis 3: 17–18):

> 'Poore banish'd Adam plowes with sweat and paine,
> The barren earth, and there in soweth graine,
> Eve fares as ill, her children she doth beare
> In grievous paine, and nurseth them in feare.'

The illustration underlines the significance of the events described in the story of Genesis for the future history of mankind. For the mid-seventeenth-century reader, Genesis explained that the earth had once been a fertile place, in which the lot of human beings had been pleasant. Human pride and sinfulness had led to the corruption of mankind, and to loss of the earth's fertility. This, in turn, forced people to labour for their food. From this historical example, it could be deduced that improvements in human morality and spirituality might go hand in hand with improvements in the cultivation of the earth, and that if the earth could be returned to something approaching its pristine fertility, mankind might be able to re-enter paradise.

Bibles

Figure 9
The seventh illustration from Nicolaes Visscher's *Figures of the Bible in Wich Almost Every History of the Holy Scriptures is Discribed*. Depicted is the plight of Adam and Eve after the Fall and their expulsion by God from paradise, from which time they had to labour for their food. Catalogue no. 7, fol. 7r.

Nicolaes Visscher (1587–1652) and his son, also Nicolaes (1618–1709), issued many different versions of Merian's engravings, with accompanying multilingual verses and texts, during the second half of the seventeenth century. Several of these appear to have circulated in England, as did separately-issued prints, for binding with Bibles, produced for the Visscher family (see catalogue no. 1).

G. E. Bentley, jr., 'Images of the Word: Separately Published English Bible Illustrations 1539–1830', *Studies in Bibliography*, vol. 47 (1994), pp. 103–28; Lucas Heinrich Wüthrich, *Das druckgraphische Werk von Matthaeus Merian d. Ae.*, vol. 3 (Hamburg, 1993), pp. 21–3; Wilco C. Poortman, *Boekzaal van de Nederlandse Bijbels* (2 vols, The Hague, 1983–86), vol. 2, pp. 56–79; Bart A. Rosier, *The Bible in Print: Netherlandish Bible Illustration in the Sixteenth Century*, trans. Chris F. Weterings (2 vols, Leiden, 1997), vol. 1, pp. 137–8.

8. *The Holy Bible Containing the Old Testament and the New*
   London, 1660
   8°: A–2Z⁸ 3A⁴
   158 × 100 mm
   Broxb. 42.9 (1)

This copy of the Authorized Version demonstrates the extent to which Bibles of the seventeenth century were the personalized products of their owners. An ordinary octavo Bible, printed by Henry Hills and John Field (who, during the Protectorate, had paid to be allowed to print Bibles in London, and who, for four years from 1660, farmed the right of the University of Oxford to print them), has been finely bound in morocco, with extensive gilt tooling, and silver corners and clasps, for its owner, Elizabeth Brodridge, whose initials 'EB' appear, worked in silver, in the centre of the front board. As well as paying a binder for this work, Elizabeth Brodridge herself has decorated the fore-edge of the Bible with a signed painting of flowers.

Bibles were objects of special meaning, which perhaps had particular importance for those who were unlikely to own many other books. Finely-bound and illustrated Bibles seem often to have belonged to women, and, in many cases, may have been gifts received on a significant occasion, such as a marriage or a birthday. Several London booksellers and binders specialized in the provision of such books.

Most of the Genesis illustrations in this Bible belong to the series engraved by van Langeren, with an accompanying Hebrew text, and Latin, Greek, and English verses supplied by Slatyer (see catalogue no. 6). Each page shows two scenes; for example, the creation of man and the naming of the animals appears above the creation of Eve, and the Ark of Noah floating on calm waters, as the raven and the dove are sent out, appears above the scene of the Ark resting on Ararat. In many of the cuts, including those of the creation of Adam and Eve, the figure of God is represented by the tetragrammaton within a shining cloud (the Shechinah). This device provided some protection against the accusations of idolatry and Popery frequently levelled at depictions of biblical scenes, and had been used from the sixteenth century to replace the figure of God when woodblocks made for Catholic works were reworked to illustrate Protestant Bibles.

T. H. Darlow and H. F. Moule, *Historical Catalogue of Printed Editions of the English Bible 1525–1961* (revised and expanded by A. S. Herbert, London, 1968), p. 206, no. 669; Diane Kelsey McColley, *A Gust for Paradise: Milton's Eden and the Visual Arts* (Urbana and Chicago, 1993), pp. 72–4 and figs. 1–12; Margaret Aston, 'The *Bishops' Bible* Illustrations', *Studies in Church History*, vol. 28 (1992), pp. 267–85.

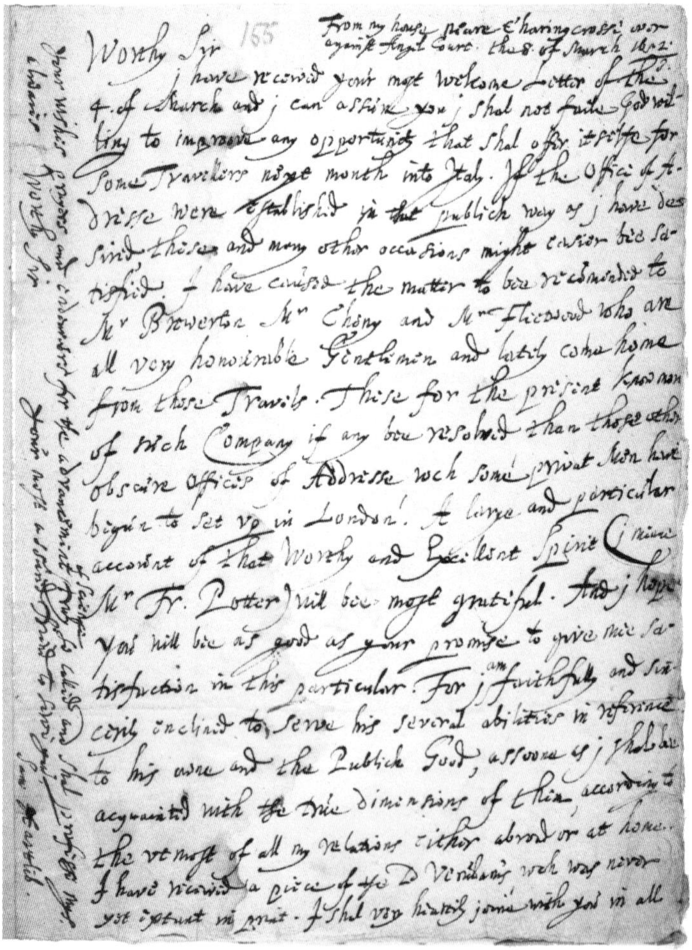

From my house neare Charingcrosse over against Angel Court. the 8. of March 1652.

Worthy Sir

I have received your most welcome Letter of the 4. of March and I can assure you I shal not faile God willing to improve any opportunity that shal offer it selfe for some Travelers next month into Italy. If the Office of Addresse were established in that publick way as I have desired those and many other occasions might easier bee satisfied. I have caused the matter to bee recommended to Mr Brewerton Mr Cheny and Mr Fleetwood who are all very honourable Gentlemen and lately come home from there Travels. These for the present know non of such Company if any bee resolved than those other obscure Offices of Addresse wch some privat Men have begun to set up in London. A large and particular account of that Worthy and Excellent Spirit (I meane Mr Fr. Potter) will bee most gratiful. And I hope you will bee as good as your promise to give mee satisfaction in this particular. For I am faithfully and sincerely inclined to serve his several abilities in reference to his owne and the Publick Good, assoone as I shal bee acquainted with the true dimensions of them, according to the utmost of all my relations either abroad or at home. I have received a piece of the L. Verulams wch was never yet extant in print. I shal very heartily joine with you in all

your wishes prayers and endeavours for the advancement of Sciences ... and shal remaine Worthy Sir Your most ... Sam: Hartlib.

Figure 10

Letter from Samuel Hartlib to John Aubrey, 8th March, 1653.
Catalogue no. 9, fol. 155r.

SAMUEL HARTLIB

Samuel Hartlib (*c.* 1600-62) was a Prussian who first came to England in the mid-1620s, when his initial contacts were with the University of Cambridge. Exiled from Germany, where the upheavals of the Thirty Years War (1618-48) made intellectual activity precarious, he made his home in England from the 1630s, settling first in Chichester, where the academy which he established soon failed, and then in London. He was deeply influenced by the utopian writings of Francis Bacon (see catalogue no. 53), and later by those of Comenius (catalogue nos. 39 and 40). Both of these authors suggested that the reform of education and philosophy might lead to universal improvement and peace, and seemed to Hartlib to offer practical solutions to the confusion and hatred which divided the contemporary Protestant Churches of Europe and left them, increasingly, at the mercy of their Catholic enemies. Although his enthusiasm for the Protestant cause seems to have fluctuated (at least to judge by the entries in his diary or commonplace book, the *Ephemerides*), Hartlib remained committed throughout his career to the extension of empirical knowledge, and the application of practical solutions to problems of the day.

From 1628, Hartlib was closely associated with John Dury (catalogue nos. 66 and 67), whose life's work consisted of trying to heal the divisions which politics and doctrine had erected between the Protestant churches of Europe. Dury shared Hartlib's belief that education and the reform of knowledge provided the means to purge minds of stubbornness and conceit. Both men were also convinced of the special nature of the times through which they were living, and persuaded by the millenarian writings of contemporary English and German divines that the sufferings of Continental Protestants were a period of trial which would eventually end in triumph.

Although Hartlib and Dury were on good terms with moderate Calvinist episcopalians within the Church of England, the meeting of the Long Parliament in London from 1641 and the establishment of the Presbyterian Westminster Assembly (see catalogue no. 71) seemed to provide them with wider opportunities to win official support for many of their schemes. It was in this context that they succeeded in bringing Comenius briefly to England. But, despite various efforts to win patronage across a broad range of activities, Hartlib never really succeeded in establishing the reformed institutions for investigation and learning after which he yearned. He did, however, bring together an increasingly varied circle of friends and correspondents who were attracted to aspects of his work. Some of the members of the Hartlib circle were individuals from whom Hartlib himself hoped to benefit, others were indigent exiles or scholars who were supported by him out of the funds which he managed to raise from government and elsewhere. Taken as a group, they provided Hartlib with a network of informants in England and across northern and central Europe, even including Ireland and North America.

The upheavals of the English Civil Wars between 1642 and 1649, and the confused political settlements which followed during the 1650s, frustrated but also encouraged Hartlib and his growing circle of correspondents. Throughout this period of dislocation, they worked tirelessly to propose ways in which poverty might be cured and the wealth of the nation increased. These were urgent matters, especially in the years around 1650, when the harvest was often poor and employment hard to find. At the same time, Hartlib and his friends searched for means to prolong and improve human life, in particular through alchemical discovery and the practice of chemical medicine, and strived to achieve dominion over nature through the application of new knowledge and new methods of understanding. As part of these quests, they developed detailed plans for co-operative scientific research, educational reform, agrarian improvement, and social amelioration. At least until the mid-1650s, they looked to those in authority as potential sponsors, appointed by God to care for his people. They were inspired by biblical promises of the restoration of human perfection at the end of time, and by the belief that contemporary wars and disasters were signs that human history was coming to its conclusion. Hartlib and his friends sought to collaborate with providence to hasten the improvement of the condition of humanity.

Despite the lack of real support for many of their schemes, several members of the Hartlib circle maintained close ties with the Commonwealth and Protectorate regimes which made it hard for them to accept the return of the Stuarts in 1660. Hartlib in particular seems to have found himself isolated by the political and ecclesiastical settlements at the Restoration. The writings of his last years are less ambitious and optimistic than before, even when referring to old friends or familiar themes. By then, Hartlib's chances of serious patronage and the opportunity to create or reform institutions had long passed. The failure of the republican experiment in England had also been a demonstration that the times were not ripe for projects such as Hartlib's.

Far from entering a new age of the rule of the saints, many of God's people found themselves condemned to live ordinary lives. Their peace of mind was undermined by the spread of heretical theologies during the 1650s, and later by the growing threat of tyranny or persecution. This was particularly true for those who were eventually unable to conform to the restored Church of England, a group which included several of the Presbyterians and Independents to whom Hartlib felt closest. Threatened by a lawsuit and, despite his protestations of loyalty, perhaps disillusioned by the likely failure of attempts to create a more inclusive church settlement, John Dury decided to go abroad again in 1661. He left, as always, in search of patronage and determined to try to keep the German Lutherans from reaching an accommodation with the Papacy.

Yet there were also several of Hartlib's friends who remained in England and felt able to participate in the new establishment. They carried a zeal for improvement into the foundation of bodies like the Royal Society and helped to shape their early activities in a practical way. The ending of a period of social, political, and religious experiment did not mean that people had ceased to trust in providence, nor that they had abandoned the hope that God might allow them to change the world they lived in for the better. It did, however, reduce the opportunity for a rapid and complete alteration of things of the kind for which Hartlib had once hoped.

Samuel Hartlib

9. Samuel Hartlib to John Aubrey, 8th March, 1653
   MS. Aubrey 12, fols. 155r–156v

John Aubrey (1626–97) first visited Samuel Hartlib in his house in Charing Cross on the 2nd December 1652. Hartlib found the young country gentleman from Wiltshire to be 'a very witty man and a mighty favorer and promoter of all Verulemian Designes' (*Hartlib Papers*, 28/2/49B [*Ephemerides*, 1652]). Both Aubrey and Hartlib shared interests in educational reform, chemical philosophy, and universal languages. They also had a number of friends in common, for example the young Robert Boyle, and would, in future, exchange information about agricultural improvement and the mechanical arts.

The exchange of information is one of the subjects of this letter from Hartlib to Aubrey, which discusses Hartlib's plans for an 'Office of Address', that is an institution for co-ordinating and analysing international correspondence which would assist in religious reformation and the advancement of learning. Hartlib had floated this idea as early as 1641, but it had taken definite shape following his discovery of the *bureau d'adresse* operated in Paris by Théophraste Renaudot. By 1646, Hartlib intended his 'Office of Address' to have two branches, for the 'Address of Accommodations' and the 'Address of Communications', and it had become the principal focus of his plans for preferment and state patronage, as well as the instrument through which he hoped to gather information that might alleviate contemporary unemployment and poverty. Although Parliament showed considerable interest in the project, especially between 1647 and 1649, no formal office was ever established, and Hartlib had to continue to rely on networks of informal correspondence, such as those referred to in this letter.

Although not found explicitly in the writings of Francis Bacon, Lord Verulam, the Office of Address was similar in conception to some of the functions of Solomon's House, described in Bacon's *New Atlantis* (1627, catalogue no. 53). Hartlib may have appeared to Aubrey to be the man most likely to fulfil Bacon's vision for the advancement of learning. Certainly, Aubrey shared much of Hartlib's interest in and esteem for Bacon's ideas, as this letter suggests. By 1655, Aubrey was himself planning to write a life of Bacon. Hartlib told John Worthington of the project enthusiastically, commenting that 'I wish he may do it to the life' (*Diary and Correspondence*, vol. 1, pp. 68–9), but Aubrey's notion of a full-scale work in the end came to nothing.

Michael Hunter, *John Aubrey and the Realm of Learning* (London, 1975), p. 44; Charles Webster (ed.), *Samuel Hartlib and the Advancement of Learning* (Cambridge, 1970), pp. 43–52; G. H. Turnbull, *Hartlib, Dury and Comenius* (Liverpool, 1947), pp. 123–4; James Crossley (ed.), *The Diary and Correspondence of Dr. John Worthington* (2 vols. in 3 parts, Manchester, 1847–86, Chetham Society, vols. 13, 36 & 114), vol. 1, pp. 68–9; *Hartlib Papers*, 17/10/1A–20B, 28/2/49B, 29/5/54A–B.

10. Samuel Hartlib (ed.)
Samuel Hartlib His Legacie: Or an
Enlargement of the Discourse of Husbandry Used in Brabant & Flaunders
2nd edition, London, 1652
4°: A-T⁴ V¹
148 × 92 mm
Ashm. 1621

Encouraged by the work of Gabriel Plattes (see catalogue no. 61), Hartlib had shown an interest in agricultural projects and improvement as early as 1639. In that year, he had become acquainted, through Plattes, with the work of the Surrey farmer, Sir Richard Weston (1591-1652), whom he called 'one of the greatest Experimenters and triers of all manner of Projects', later describing him as 'a Papist but of a free and communicative disposition and one of the greatest husbandmen in all England'.

In 1644, Weston, who had already pioneered the growing of clover and other improvements on his lands in Surrey, travelled to the Low Countries, following the sequestration of his estates in England by Parliament. On his journey, he saw how new crops, and new methods of tillage and of rotation, could generate significant profits from otherwise redundant soils. The following year, he composed *A Discours of Husbandrie Used in Brabant and Flanders*, in the form of 'a legacy to his sons'. This work, which encouraged the use of clover, root crops, and hemp, to prepare the soil for wheat and barley, and which envisaged the profitable sale of crops at market, came to Hartlib's attention, in the form of a faulty manuscript copy, procured through Robert Boyle. It was published by Hartlib in 1650.

By then, Hartlib had become especially concerned with problems of unemployment and poverty in England, and with the need for intensive husbandry, cheaper produce, and improved yields to help combat them. Initially, he was unaware of the identity of the author whose treatise he had published, but, by December 1650, he began to suspect that it was by Weston, and obtained a better copy of the manuscript. Correspondence with Weston followed, leading to the publication by Hartlib in 1652 of an enlarged and corrected version of the *Discours*. Spurred on by Weston's example, Hartlib decided himself to make 'a Legacie of the same kinde to this Common-wealth' (Hartlib to Weston, 2nd May 1651, printed in [Weston], pp. 28-9).

Hartlib's *Legacie* (first published in 1651, and enlarged in both 1652 and 1655) built on Weston's discoveries by deploying the knowledge of techniques of improvement which could be gleaned from Hartlib's wide circle of correspondents. Among these, the most important were Robert Child (d. 1654), a chemist and Kentish man, who had visited New England but was, by 1651, resident in Ireland, and Arnold Boate (see catalogue nos. 63, 64 and 79), who had been physician to the English forces in Ireland, and was now resident in Paris. Child contributed a long letter on the deficiencies of English husbandry, whilst Boate added an appendix of his letters concerning husbandry (which helped to clarify such matters as the cultivation of sainfoin and lucerne), and an 'interrogatory' relating to the husbandry of Ireland – a Baconian questionnaire which discussed Irish natural history in general.

Although it was often confusing, Hartlib's *Legacie* generated considerable debate about the best methods of agricultural improvement. Implementation of Hartlib's recommendations was often frustrated by difficulties in obtaining seeds or equipment, but his work encouraged others to believe that yields could be raised, and people fed and employed, without depleting natural resources. It suggested that these benefits could be achieved through the hard work of right-minded individuals. As such, it seemed to offer the hope that the fertility of the earth could be restored to its original extent by a virtuous few, a biblical motif which was taken up by other agrarian writers in the Hartlib circle.

One right-minded individual who was particularly interested by Hartlib's *Legacie* was John Aubrey, whose signature appears at the top of the title-page of this copy. Aubrey's annotations suggest that he was particularly intrigued by the interrogatory relating to Ireland, to which he added fresh information, perhaps during his stay in Ireland in 1661.

G. E. Fussell, *The Old English Farming Books from Fitzherbert to Tull 1523–1730* (London, 1947), pp. 41-4; [Richard Weston], *A Discours of Husbandrie used in Brabant and Flanders*, edited by Samuel Hartlib (3rd edition, London, 1654); Charles Webster, *The Great Instauration* (London, 1975), pp. 46, 431-3, & 471-4; Joan Thirsk, 'Agricultural Innovations and their Diffusion', pp. 533-89 in Joan Thirsk (ed.), *The Agrarian History of England and Wales, Volume V, 1640–1750, Part II: Agrarian Change* (Cambridge, 1985), p. 549; A. R. Michell, 'Sir Richard Weston and the Spread of Clover Cultivation', *Agricultural History Review*, vol. 22 (1974), pp. 160-1; Mauro Ambrosoli, *The Wild and the Sown*, translated by Mary McCann Salvatorelli (Cambridge, 1997), pp. 305-15; Michael Hunter, *John Aubrey and the Realm of Learning* (London, 1975), pp. 36-7; *Hartlib Papers*, 8/7/1A-2B, 15/4/11A-B, 28/2/7B, 28/2/10A, 30/4/21A, 30/5/1A-10B, 31/20/1A-4B, 46/7/9A-10B, 46/7/13A-14B.

11. Samuel Hartlib (ed.)
A Designe for Plentie by an Universall Planting
of Fruit-Trees: Tendred by Some Wel-Wishers to the Publick
London, [1652]
4°: A–D⁴
152 × 90 mm
Ashm. 1065(23)

By the 1650s, many writers had expressed concern about the state of England's woodlands, and the danger that the country would experience a timber famine, with disastrous consequences for trade and national security, as well as for industry and individual welfare. In Hartlib's *Legacie*, Robert Child had written about the need for legislation to protect existing woods and forests, and to encourage replanting. He had also taken up Gabriel Plattes' suggestion that landowners should plant trees, especially fruit trees, in hedgerows, and among the crops in the fields. Other contemporary agricultural improvers, notably Walter Blith (see catalogue no. 15), discussed similar remedies for the shortage of timber, and were optimistic about the profits which might arise from them. In 1652, Hartlib had made contact with Ralph Austen (see catalogue no. 14), whose work on fruit trees and orchards he intended to publish. Perhaps because of delays with the production of that book, Hartlib brought out *A Designe for Plentie*, which functioned in part as an advertisement for Austen's longer work.

A Designe for Plentie was the work of a Norfolk minister, from Lothingland, and had been communicated to Hartlib by Colonel John Barkstead, governor of Yarmouth, and subsequently of the Tower of London. It promised plenty to the poor from the planting of the commons and wastelands with fruit trees, which would transform them into a new garden of God. Both Hartlib's preface and the tract itself expressly drew attention to the providential origins of the calling of husbandman, and suggested that God's goodness would ensure success for those who returned to that activity. They thus referred back to the historical example of Genesis, in which Adam had tended the fruit trees in Eden, before labouring more strenuously at tillage after the Fall and his expulsion from

Samuel Hartlib

paradise. Such reference was made explicit in the quotation printed on the title-page (Genesis 1: 29, not Genesis 1: 20, as printed):

> And God said, Behold, I have given you every herb bearing seed, which is upon the face of all the earth, and every tree, in the which is the fruit of a tree yielding seed; to you it shall be for meat.

This copy of Hartlib's *Designe for Plentie* belonged to John Aubrey (see catalogue nos. 9 and 10), who shared Hartlib's interest in agricultural improvement, and recorded developments in his native Wiltshire. In 1652, Aubrey had mentioned to Hartlib a novel method of threshing which he had invented, but which he wished to keep secret in order not to harm the employment of the poor.

Charles Webster, *The Great Instauration* (London, 1975), pp. 477–8; Joan Thirsk, 'Agricultural Innovations and their Diffusion', pp. 533–89 in Joan Thirsk (ed.), *The Agrarian History of England and Wales, Volume V, 1640–1750, Part II: Agrarian Change* (Cambridge, 1985), p. 550; Blanche Henrey, *British Botanical and Horticultural Literature Before 1800* (3 vols, London, 1975), vol. 1, p. 169; *Hartlib Papers*, 28/2/49B, 41/1/2A–17B.

12. Samuel Hartlib (ed.)
The Reformed Husband-Man; Or a Brief Treatise of the Errors, Defects, and Inconveniences of our English Husbandry
2nd issue, London, 1651
4°: A² B⁴ C³
163 × 98 mm
Vet. A3 e. 597

The text of *The Reformed Husband-man* was communicated to Hartlib three years before its publication, and was perhaps written by Cressy Dymock (catalogue no. 62). Its principal concern was the English habit of ploughing too deeply and leaving furrows which were too broad, leading to the waste of seed. The author was worried about the shortage of pasture and woodland, and hoped that improved methods of ploughing and sowing might release land for these purposes and for the poor. Writing in the context of a succession of bad harvests between 1648 and 1651, the author hoped that publication would encourage Parliamentary support for his plans and raise money to make practical his vision of a new distribution of farming lands and a new method of ploughing.

Both the anonymous tract, and its preface, which was written by Hartlib, argued that the current situation in England presented a providential opportun-

Samuel Hartlib

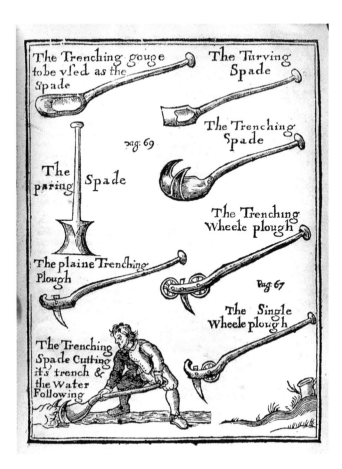

Figure 11
This illustration, from Walter Blith's *English Improver Improved*, shows a variety of different tools for digging and ploughing. Use of hoes and other devices would alleviate the waste associated with the English habit of ploughing land too deeply and assist in reducing it to 'pristine fertility'. Catalogue no. 15, facing p. 68.

ity for agricultural reform. In part, this was simply a reflection on the volatility of contemporary affairs, in particular in the land market. But it also demonstrated the belief of Hartlib and his friends that husbandry was a God-given activity, which might be enhanced providentially at the moment of greatest need for God's people. Thus, Hartlib comments in the preface that husbandry is 'the most profitable *Industry* unto *Humane Society*; wherein the *Providence*, the *Power*, the *Wisdom* and the *Goodness* of *God*, appears unto man more eminently then in any other way of *Industry* whatsoever' (sig. A2 verso).

G. E. Fussell, *The Old English Farming Books from Fitzherbert to Tull 1523–1730* (London, 1947), p. 45.

Figure 12

Adam and Eve tending the Garden of Eden.
Under God's gaze the Garden is bringing forth plenty. Adam gathers fruit and Eve herbs, while in the background the mythical 'vegetable' lamb – which grew and propagated like a plant – grazes.
Catalogue no. 20, title-page.

THE GARDEN

During the seventeenth century, Protestant theologians encouraged people to read the Bible literally and as a coherent historical narrative. In this narrative, the events which took place in the Garden of Eden defined the rest of the course of human history. The outline of the story related in the opening three chapters of Genesis can be given relatively briefly. God had created the first man (Adam) and woman (Eve), and placed them in paradise, where it was their task to look after the Garden. They lived in an environment of pristine natural fertility and peace. All this was altered when the man and the woman sinned (the Fall), by disobeying God and eating the fruit of the tree of knowledge of good and evil. As a consequence of the Fall, Adam and Eve were expelled from paradise and forced to fend for themselves. The earth became corrupted and harder to till for food. Women were punished by the pains of childbirth, and death overshadowed all people. At the same time, God promised future redemption for humanity through Christ.

Although the basic narrative was easy to establish, the meaning of the events which had taken place in the Garden was often the subject of debate in the seventeenth century. To a considerable extent, the way in which scripture was understood depended on the theological assumptions of the interpreter. Nowhere was this more true than in the interpretation of the Fall. Many early-modern English readers of the Bible followed the teaching of Theodore Beza (building on the work of John Calvin), and believed that the proper understanding of God's nature, in particular of his divine

The Garden

foreknowledge of events, demanded the predestination of human nature, and the division of people into the inherently righteous and the inherently sinful. According to this view, the seed of both the elect and the damned could be found in Adam; his original sin clouded the nature and lives of all human beings, but was atoned for in the elect by Christ's sacrifice.

Most members of the Hartlib circle believed in some version of this theology, and were also persuaded by the biblical criticism of reformed scholastic theologians, who argued that the teaching of Calvin and Beza was fully compatible with a literal interpretation of scripture and with the understanding of the events of Genesis given by the first Christian writers, in particular in the Epistles of St Paul. However, over the course of the seventeenth century, English readers of the Bible became increasingly familiar with alternative interpretations of the text of the Bible and of the teachings of both the early Christians and the first generation of reformed theologians. In particular, the belief that Adam's sin had been imputed to all future human beings came to be challenged, as did the view that Christ had died for the elect alone. Irrespective of which tradition they came from, seventeenth-century English interpreters of Genesis stressed the liberty of Adam's actions and the role of human free will in the Fall. For traditional Calvinists, however, the Fall had led to human bondage to sin and death, and the effective loss of the ability to act with pristine freedom. The recovery of this liberty could only be achieved through God's preservation of his saints, and his providential guidance of their affairs.

If the actions of Adam and Eve provided material for the prehistory of free will, then several other aspects of the story of Genesis were used by early modern readers to explain the origins of human nature and practices. Adam was considered by many to be a type of Christ; more controversially, he was thought by some to be the original monarch who had been given dominion over the world by God. Mid-seventeenth-century English readers disagreed about such questions as whether Adam's rule had been conditional on his labour; whether property had initially been held in common; whether the dominion which Adam had could be passed on by inheritance; and whether Adam's example embodied the proper authority due in the future to all monarchs and to the fathers of all human families. The answers which they gave were often either inspirations for or reflections on their own political stances, especially as they were forced to choose between King and Parliament in the 1640s.

Debate also focussed on the meaning of Genesis' account of Eve for the future status of women. Although many orthodox authors wished to stress Adam's responsibility for human sin, others regarded Eve as most culpable. Eve was characterized variously as weaker than Adam, and therefore more easily deceived into sin, or as Adam's equal in knowledge and thus as the real perpetrator of his fall. Many interpreters wished to argue that Genesis justified a subordinate status for women, either through the inferior creation of Eve, or through her being punished, after the Fall, by being made subject to Adam's authority. The second, more historical, interpretation perhaps won wider favour. Critics of Eve were, however, careful to preserve the prophetic identification of her with the future Church of Christ.

By and large, such complex interpretations did not feature in the writings of members of the Hartlib circle, which were more concerned with the practical examples to be derived from a literal and historical reading of Genesis. Even when reference was made to the political meaning of Adam's rule, it was turned to provide a justification for the contemporary pursuit of improvement. Writing to his uncle, John Beale (see catalogue no. 17), in 1657, Peter Smith referred to God's punishment of Adam, and his sentence in Genesis 3: 19 that 'in the sweat of thy face shalt thou eat bread' (*Hartlib Papers*, 52/20A–21B):

> w[ch] indeed, though it was a punishment to Adam, yet is it the best nurse of health, & chearfullnesse to his posterity: And I suppose that if great conquerours, & troublers of the world were but sensible of those pure & naturall delights of eating the fruits of their owne planting & living upon their owne labours, or in a higher sphear were capable of the joy that ariseth from such actions that benefitt the publick without hurt to any particular, such as are the invention of the plow, planting of fruit, dreining of Fens etc. they would acknowledge their glory to be very partiall, & their great joyes to be attended with intervals of trouble & remorse in comparison of these.

For Hartlib and his friends, as well as for many other seventeenth-century readers, the most important meanings of the story of the Garden could be found in the account of history which it gave and in the lessons which it taught about human behaviour. Thus, the opening chapters of Genesis contained information about the original human condition and the potential which human beings had had before the Fall. They revealed that Adam and Eve had always been intended to work (to dress the Garden) but that labour had not always been onerous or difficult. They showed that the human mind, when it was not encumbered by sin, had the capacity to understand the natural world and to comprehend the essences of things from the observation of their appearances. Such a capacity had enabled Adam to name all the creatures of the earth (Genesis 2: 19–20), using, it was supposed, a language which united words and things.

Information drawn from apocryphal writings and from Jewish tradition further suggested that Adam had once possessed a deep knowledge of the workings of

The Garden

the universe, which had been communicated to him by God. This true and complete natural theology had been the basis for the pious acts of worship which Adam and Eve had performed in paradise before they fell, and which are described at length in accounts of Eden such as that given in Milton's *Paradise Lost* (catalogue no. 68). Although most critics argued that the Fall had occurred on the evening of the sixth day, before the sun had set on the creation of man, they nonetheless believed that Adam in his innocency had possessed a special knowledge of God and his actions.

The most important lesson which had to be drawn from the Fall was the need to be obedient to God and to his providential decrees. Satan, whom commentators depicted as having entered the body of a serpent in the Garden and given it a voice with which to tempt Eve, was always on hand to repeat the deception with which he had encouraged the first human beings to sin. Yet devout people might overcome Satan's wiles, and in the process recover some of the lost knowledge which Adam had once possessed. The hope of members of the Hartlib circle was that, in the last days, it might be possible to restore the fertility which the earth had lost after the Fall through the practice of a scientific husbandry, which also paid attention to the spiritual duties of the farmer or gardener that Adam had neglected at the moment of his sin. Observation and the compilation of experimental knowledge would help to achieve this, as well as to restore the lost wisdom of Adam. Chemical researches, such as those undertaken by Ralph Austen (see catalogue no. 14), Benjamin Worsley, and the young Robert Boyle, might begin to establish which element made plants grow, or provide substances to heal human illnesses. Experiment and innovation would perhaps restore the earth's lost fruitfulness as well as providing the liberating activity of labour for England's poor. This good work could expect divine support since a number of biblical prophecies seemed to suggest that God would restore lost knowledge and plenty to the saints at the end of time.

The millenarian context was important for improvers like Hartlib and his friends. As Calvinists, they did not believe that human beings could bring about their own salvation. Indeed, one of the lessons of Eden was that the covenant of works, under which Adam and Eve had originally been placed, represented an impossible route to heaven. Only the covenant of grace which God had subsequently made with his elect could promise redemption, although it also placed a heavy burden of obedience on the believer. Part of that burden could be relieved by collaboration with providence in the improvement of the world, once the time was ripe. The apocalyptic expectation under which they lived helped to encourage members of the Hartlib circle to adopt practical interpretations of the Bible. Perhaps surprisingly, given their interest in Comenius's philosophy (see catalogue nos. 39 and 40), they seem in

Figure 13

One of the mechanical devices illustrated by John Wilkins in his *Mathematicall Magick*. It consisted of a wind-vane connected to a series of gears and a pulley, and allowed the whole weight of an oak to be lifted by a slight force, such as the human breath. Mechanical devices were a source of continual interest for proponents of the new experimental philosophy of the 17th century. Placed within a long tradition of practical mathematics, they were entirely consistent with the 'mathematicall' aspect in the title of Wilkins' work, as well as the perceived need to deploy mechanical aids in agriculture. Such devices, it was argued, would help to restore man's dominion over nature lost at the Fall. Catalogue no. 19, p. 98.

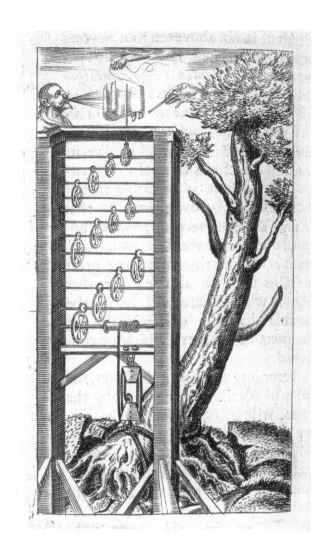

the end to have largely rejected more mystical readings of the Bible, such as those to be found in the contemporary English translations of the work of Jacob Boehme. Their view of Genesis was governed by a sense of history. Accordingly, they were receptive to the idea that Eden had been a real place which could be located geographically. They believed that the events that had taken place in the Garden had begun the process of human history, which might be about to end in their lifetimes. The notion of a return to Eden inspired their work, which was intended to improve mankind spiritually as well as materially.

The Garden

13. Sir Hugh Plat
    The Garden of Eden
    London, 1653
    8°: a⁸ A-K⁸
    119 × 68 mm
    CR. R. 62

Sir Hugh Plat (1552–1608) was the son of a wealthy London brewer and devoted himself to mechanical inventions, agriculture, and distilling during a long career of projects for the public good. He conducted horticultural trials on his estate at Bethnal Green, and corresponded extensively with farmers and gardeners. He also carried out chemical experiments, and collected recipes and novelties. He compiled a number of books of secrets (see catalogue no. 64), containing both practical and curious information. Plat was knighted in 1605, but despite this he had difficulty winning wider support for his schemes for improvement. In 1608, a work of his on gardening, entitled *Floraes Paradise*, was published. It clearly did not sell well, since the sheets were reissued with a cancel title-page in 1653. This prompted the owner of Plat's manuscript, Charles Bellingham, to publish a new edition of the work, now called *The Garden of Eden*, including material which had been omitted from the first printing. *The Garden of Eden* was reprinted in 1655 and 1659, and reissued with a previously unpublished second part in 1660.

Both *Floraes Paradise* and *The Garden of Eden* consist largely of an analysis of the different sorts of fruit, flowers, herbs, and trees which may be grown by the assiduous gardener. They both give instructions on how to grow and propagate different types of plants. In addition, *The Garden of Eden* also includes Plat's discussion of a 'philosophical garden'. This draws on the work of occult writers like Cornelius Agrippa of Nettesheim and Joseph Duchesne, and depicts the plants of the garden in mystical, possibly alchemical, imagery.

The re-publication of Plat's work in the 1650s demonstrate the hunger for ways of achieving agricultural improvement at that time, and underline the difficulty of diffusing new ideas and establishing new practices in the early seventeenth century. Plat's writings were valued for their compendiousness, and also for their accuracy, brevity, and clarity. The fact that Plat had himself tried many of his horticultural suggestions experimentally made his advice particularly valuable. John Beale, the Herefordshire agricultural improver and enthusiast for the virtues of cider (see catalogue no. 17), told Hartlib that: 'Sir H. Plats garden of Eden is written without pompe. I would I could see another like collection of later discoveryes. Sometimes from five lines in him, I could deduce hundreds of pretty experiments' (Beale to Hartlib, 15th November 1659, *Hartlib*

Papers, 62/25/1A-4B). However, although some of Hartlib's correspondents were intrigued by the chemical learning displayed in Plat's 'philosophical garden', others derided it as 'a meere Sphinx not to bee understood without a Oedipus' (Henry Jenney to Hartlib, 28th September 1657, *Hartlib Papers*, 53/35/3A-4B). The imagery of the Garden of Eden was primarily an inspiration for agricultural labour and improvement to the members of the Hartlib circle, rather than a device encoding occult knowledge. They read the story of Genesis in literal and historical terms, rather than in those of mystery and allegory.

Bent Juel-Jensen, 'Plat's Floraes Paradise – Garden of Eden – 1608/1653', *The Book Collector*, vol. 38 (1989), pp. 406-7; William Eamon, *Science and the Secrets of Nature* (Princeton, 1994), pp. 311-14; Charles F. Mullett, 'Hugh Plat: Elizabethan Virtuoso', in Charles T. Prouty (ed.) *Studies in Honor of A. H. R. Fairchild* (University of Missouri Studies, vol. 21, 1946), pp. 91-118; *Hartlib Papers*, 28/1/60B-71A, 53/35/3A-4B, 62/25/1A-4B.

14. Ralph Austen
The Spirituall Use, of an Orchard; or Garden of Fruit-Trees
Oxford, 1653
4°: π¹ *⁴ 2*² ¶-3¶⁴ A-M⁴ P-T⁴
156 × 100 mm
Antiq. e. E. 1653.1

In February 1652, Ralph Austen (*c.* 1612-76) made contact with Samuel Hartlib, seeking the publication of a book on fruit trees which he was preparing, and expressing the hope that Parliament might give its support to it. Austen was a practising nurseryman, who had grown up in Leek in Staffordshire, but had been based in Oxford since 1646. A keen supporter of religious and political reformation, whose mother was a cousin of Henry Ireton, Austen acted as a secretary to the Parliamentarian Visitors of the University of Oxford from 1648, and was appointed their registrar in 1650. He was thus closely involved with the expulsion of opponents of the new settlements in church and state from the University, and with the continued monitoring of educational standards and political obedience there.

During the 1650s, Austen kept a small nursery in Oxford, but his plans to enclose part of Shotover forest in 1655 failed because he lacked the capital necessary to buy out the rights of local commoners. Thereafter, he unsuccessfully sought the patronage of Major-General Fleetwood, having petitioned Parliament to promote the planting of fruit trees just before the death of Cromwell in 1658. Austen set up a cider factory in Oxford in 1659, and made

The Garden

Figure 14
The engraved frontispiece of *A Treatise of Fruit-Trees* by Ralph Austen – 'Practiser in ye Art of Planting'. From catalogue no. 14.

a living through his continuing activites as a gardener, planter, and nurseryman. As well as corresponding about fruit trees, Austen shared the more general concern of many members of the Hartlib circle that new crops and horticultural practices should alleviate poverty and unemployment.

Austen's practical experience as a nurseryman made his reactions to the growing literature of improvement particularly interesting to Hartlib, and the two men corresponded extensively in 1652 and 1653 about the progress of Austen's *Treatise of Fruit-Trees*, which was eventually published in June 1653, together with *The Spiritual Use of an Orchard*. In the copy here, the two works are bound together, as the signatures of their sheets suggest they were supposed to be. It seems likely that they were printed simultaneously; certainly, the delay in publication was caused by problems with the engraving of the frontispiece, rather than by the author or printer. As late as May 1653, Austen was complaining to Hartlib about the difficulties he was having with John Goddard, the engraver who was supposed to cut a brass plate for the title-page. Some resolution must have been achieved, however, since Goddard's name signs the finished engraving of an enclosed orchard and garden, which follows Austen's original design. The title-page refers to the Song of Solomon 4: 12-13, 'A garden inclosed is my sister, my spouse; a spring shut up, a fountain sealed. Thy plants are an orchard of pomegranates, with pleasant fruits'; it is set beneath a device which shows profits shaking hands with pleasures.

The iconography of the frontispiece is taken up in the themes of Austen's text. This describes the propagation and care of fruit trees, and the benefits which will accrue to the Commonwealth from keeping them. Its experimental and horticultural discussions are accompanied by extensive spiritual meditations, which may be drawn from trees and from orchards to improve the soul of the husbandman. Austen's *Treatise of Fruit-Trees* was dedicated to Hartlib, and included extensive comment on modern books of husbandry which Hartlib had sent to its author (such as Blith's *English Improver Improved*, see catalogue no. 15), as well as discussion of classical agriculture. It argued that the true, ancient husbandry had not consisted simply of tillage, but had also included horticulture, which had been Adam's original employment in Eden, before 'he was put away from this worke to till the ground, a lower and inferior labour' (sig. ¶4 recto). Viticulture had been restored by Noah, Austen argued, and the Bible provided plenty of historical examples of the advantages of growing plants and trees. Such activity was profitable and it also generated fruit which was beneficial to health. Moreover, the husbandman in his orchard had constant opportunity to meditate on the Fall and on original sin, 'whereof we were all guilty *in such a Place*' (p. 32), encouraging him to turn his skills and his profits to the public good.

In Austen's writings, the teachings of the book of nature (the spiritualized orchard) and of the book of scripture are shown to be in close harmony. Biblical history is deployed to justify a particular approach to improvement, and to suggest that bodies and souls, as well as material conditions, can be returned to a paradisical state through prudent and devout activity.

Falconer Madan, *Oxford Books: a Bibliography of Printed Works Relating to the University and City of Oxford* (3 vols, Oxford, 1895-1931), vol. 3, pp. 26-27; Charles Webster, *The Great Instauration* (London, 1975), pp. 477-80 & 546-8; James Turner, 'Ralph Austen, an Oxford Horticulturalist of the Seventeenth Century', *Garden History*, vol. 6 (1978), pp. 39-45; Montagu Burrows (ed.), *The Register of the Visitors of the University of Oxford, from A.D. 1647 to A.D. 1658* (Camden Society, New Series, vol. 29, 1881); *Hartlib Papers*, 41/1/2A-13B, 41/1/26A-29B, 41/1/96A-97B, 41/1/114A-115B, 41/1/121A-122B, 41/1/146A-B, 57/5/5A-B.

The Garden

15. Walter Blith
 The English Improver Improved or the Survey of Husbandry Surveyed
 3rd impression, London, 1652
 4°: π² A⁴ a-e⁴ f² B-2I⁴ χ¹ 2K-2N⁴ 2O² (with 4 plates)
 152 × 90 mm
 Vet. A3 e. 1430

First published in 1649, Blith's *English Improver* was one of the most important contemporary handbooks for agricultural improvement. It was reprinted in the same year, and an emended and enlarged edition, *The English Improver Improved*, was published in 1652, and reprinted the next year. Walter Blith (d. 1652) was a gentleman of Cotesbach in Leicestershire, who served as a captain in the Parliamentary armies, mainly in the midlands. There, he was also an agent for the sequestration of Royalist land. Between 1649 and 1650, he was engaged in the survey of crown lands, some of which he purchased in Potterspury, Northamptonshire. He may also have acquired land in the Lincolnshire fens; certainly, he seems to have gained a detailed knowledge of drainage techniques between 1649 and 1652.

Blith's original work was addressed to both houses of Parliament, and described the main legal, social, and technical obstacles faced by agricultural improvers, as well as setting out six ways in which the ordinary farmer could improve his land. These were largely standard techniques of land management and fertilization. *The English Improver* already demonstrated Blith's concern about social constraints on good farming practice, for example the tendency to overstock the commons, and the years 1649 to 1652 provided plenty of opportunity for Blith to observe the consequences, in terms of food shortages, high prices, and unemployment, generated by social dislocation, bad weather, and the inadequate use of land. *The English Improver Improved* included discussions of new crops, like clover, sainfoin, and lucerne, woad, weld and madder, hops, saffron and liquorice, rape, cole-seed, hemp, and flax, as well as discussions of how to plant orchard and garden fruits. Blith also expanded his discussions of drainage techniques and methods of ploughing, and included illustrations of different types of plough and spade, and of a device for raising water.

The English Improver Improved also boasted a new frontispiece, which depicted warring Royalists and Parliamentarians beating their swords into ploughshares (as instructed in Isaiah 2: 4) in much the way that Blith himself had done. Under the arms of the Commonwealth, and a banner proclaiming 'Vive la re publick', it showed the action of the trenching spade, used for constructing drainage trenches, a plough team, a man using a level for surveying, and a collection of other useful tools (a pick, a trenching gouge, a turving spade, and an English

The Garden

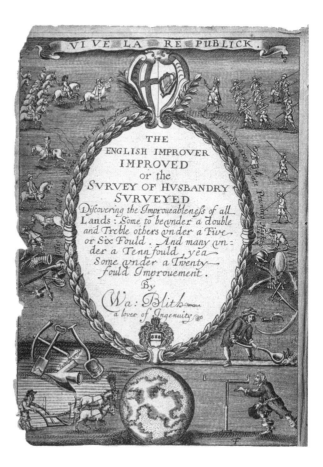

Figure 15

The frontispiece of Blith's *English Improver Improved*. Blith depicts a range of tools and practical activities associated with husbandry, under an illustration of Royalist and Parliamentarian troops, of whom some are shown beating their swords into the shape of ploughshares. From catalogue no. 15.

ploughshare). All of these were described at greater length in the text, as well as being illustrated in greater detail. In his enlarged work, Blith also paid tribute to 'my good friend M. Samuell Hurtlip' (sig. C3 recto), and added his voice to that of Robert Child (in Hartlib's *Legacie*, catalogue no. 10), criticizing the deficiencies of contemporary English husbandry and agricultural writing. Blith's book was much taken up within the Hartlib circle. His ideas about orchards and fruit trees helped to encourage Ralph Austen in his work (to which Blith himself alluded); Cressy Dymock (see catalogue no. 62) enquired about Blith's success in using turnips as fodder for cattle; both Child and Dymock discussed Blith's techniques for drainage, and John Beale sought out trees whose wood could be used to make Blith's trenching plough. At least until the Restoration, *The English Improver Improved* was therefore one of the most successful manuals for husbandry.

Although Blith couched much of his work in the secular terms of profit and improvement, and was often harsh in his discussions of the causes of poverty, both *The English Improver* and its sequel also carried a spiritual message. 'Improvement', the running head in both works asserted, was the 'Reducement of Land to pristine Fertility'. The labour of agriculture was a way to redeem people from idleness and debauchery, the historical means which God had given man to alleviate the barrenness of the earth. Only the continued apostasy of human beings, and their false pride in their own achievements and traditions, Blith argued, prevented people from embracing improvements wholeheartedly: 'were ingenuitie the Fashion of the Times, This Kingdom would be the Paradice of the World' (*English Improver*, sig. a2 recto).

To counteract such errors, Blith held up the examples of biblical husbandmen and improvers, from Adam to Solomon, as well as that of God himself, 'the great Husbandman' (*English Improver*, p. 4) who had first made plants and trees come forth upon the earth. God intended the preservation of his creation, Blith suggested, and mankind was the instrument by which he would achieve this. For Blith, therefore, the historical examples of the Bible taught the lesson that individuals had a duty to God to practise a reformed husbandry, and that only by doing this might their country be redeemed from sin, famine, and warfare into a new Eden of peace and plenty.

G. E. Fussell, *The Old English Farming Books from Fitzherbert to Tull 1523–1730* (London, 1947), pp. 52-3; Charles Webster, *The Great Instauration* (London, 1975), pp. 469-83; Joan Thirsk, 'Plough and Pen: Agricultural Writers in the Seventeenth Century', in T. H. Aston, P. R. Coss, Christopher Dyer, and Joan Thirsk (eds.), *Social Relations and Ideas* (Cambridge, 1983), pp. 295-318; Andrew McRae, *God Speed the Plough: The Representation of Agrarian England, 1500–1660* (Cambridge, 1996), pp. 161-5 & 226-8; Simon Schaffer, 'The Earth's Fertility as a Social Fact in Early Modern England', in Mikuláš Teich, Roy Porter, and Bo Gustafsson (eds.), *Nature and Society in Historical Context* (Cambridge, 1997), pp. 124-47; *Hartlib Papers*, 15/5/12A-13B, 28/2/63A, 41/1/8A-13B, 52/162A-65B, 55/21/3A-4B, 66/23/1A-2B.

16. John Evelyn
Prospectus for Elysium Britannicum
MS. Rawl. A. 185, fol. 40

This broadside prospectus for a book which would cover theoretical and historical aspects of gardening, garden design, and horticulture was circulated by Evelyn to his friends before 1660. The copy described here was endorsed by Samuel Pepys, to whom Evelyn read sections from the manuscript of the *Elysium* in November 1665. Although the publication of Evelyn's work was announced in 1669, the completed book never extricated itself from the vast and incoherent mass of Evelyn's *Elysium* manuscript.

The Garden

John Evelyn (1620–1706) spent most of the 1640s travelling on the Continent, living in exile in Paris for three years from 1649. On his return to England in 1652, he had little chance of the public employment for which his education and rank had fitted him, because of his Royalist sympathies. Instead, he retired to Sayes Court at Deptford, where he planted a garden of trees and indulged his interests and tastes as a virtuoso.

Evelyn first came to the attention of Samuel Hartlib in 1653, when he was engaged on collecting material for a history of trades, a project which he would pursue later in his life, particularly as a Fellow of the Royal Society in the 1660s. Despite his Baconian interests, Evelyn's political and religious sympathies kept him at a distance from many of the schemes of the Hartlib circle. He visited Hartlib for the first time in December 1655, to discuss beekeeping, but his most productive contact among Hartlib's friends was John Beale (see catalogue no. 17). In 1658, Evelyn had produced a translation of Nicholas de Bonnefons' *The French Gardiner* (an idea first mooted by Arnold Boate, see catalogue nos. 63 and 79), and, by 1659, he had drawn up a synopsis for his own book on gardening, which he circulated in Oxford and elsewhere. Writing to John Worthington on 30th January 1660, Hartlib remarked that 'when Mr. Evelyn's Book conc.[erning] Gardens will be finished, he will like it far better than his Garden near London' (*Diary and Correspondence*, vol. 1, p. 174).

A copy of the synopsis also reached Beale in Herefordshire, who remarked on the extent of Evelyn's knowledge of modern ideas about horticulture. He suggested that Evelyn should extend his proposed book by a further six or seven chapters, on topics such as garden entertainments, the hybridization of flowers, and, in particular, mounts and prospects. Beale's response to Evelyn's synopsis included a lengthy discussion (subsequently interpolated into Evelyn's *Elysium* manuscript) of his plans to create a garden around the site of an ancient British settlement on Backbury Hill, near Ledbury, Herefordshire, inspired by Evelyn's proposals and by his own conviction that the true, ancient gardening had made use of natural, rather than man-made, features, such as the prospects available from the tops of hills.

Both Beale and Evelyn believed that the proper art of gardening involved a return to biblical and ancient practices. In his extensive correspondence with Evelyn, Beale regularly drew attention to the works of classical authors on gardens, and to historical examples drawn from the Bible. He looked forward confidently to the location of the true site of paradise, and the rediscovery of the original language of Eden (which he thought might be Chinese). For his part, Evelyn began his *Elysium* manuscript with a discussion of the expulsion of Adam and Eve from Eden and of their subsequent rediscovery of gardening and husbandry, arguing that 'God had destin'd them this employment for a sweete & most agreable punition of their sinns' (Evelyn Papers Ms. 45, facing p. 1). Evelyn was confident that human ingenuity and labour could return the earth to its pristine fertility and beauty, and restore paradise in a garden designed according to ancient precepts (Evelyn Papers Ms. 45, p. 1):

> Adam instructed his Posteritie how to handle the Spade so dextrously, that, in processe of tyme, men began, with the indulgence of heaven, to recover that by Arte and Industrie, which was before produced to them spontaneously; and to improve the Fruites of the Earth, to gratifie as well their pleasures and contemplations, as their necessities and daily foode.

Like others of Hartlib's acquaintance, Evelyn hoped that new and rediscovered techniques of gardening and husbandry might restore the fertility of the earth, which had been lost at the Fall. However, Evelyn placed less stress on the material benefits which might result from such a restoration, and more on the spiritual advantages of gardens, calling attention to the perfect knowledge of Adam in Eden, and arguing that the gardener might be 'an absolute Philosopher' (Evelyn Papers Ms. 45, p. 4).

Geoffrey Keynes, *John Evelyn: A Study in Bibliophily with a Bibliography of his Writings* (2nd edition, Oxford, 1968), p. 236; *John Evelyn in the British Library* (London, 1995), pp. 27–8; Michael Hunter, 'John Evelyn in the 1650s: A Virtuoso in Quest of a Role', in Michael Hunter, *Science and the Shape of Orthodoxy* (Woodbridge, 1995), pp. 66–98; Charles Webster, *The Great Instauration* (London, 1975), p. 427; Peter H. Goodchild, '"No Phantasticall Utopia, but a Reall Place": John Evelyn, John Beale and Backbury Hill, Herefordshire', *Garden History*, vol. 19 (1991), pp. 105–27; Graham Parry, 'John Evelyn as Hortulan Saint', in Michael Leslie and Timothy Raylor (eds.), *Culture and Cultivation in Early Modern England* (Leicester, 1992), pp. 130–50; Michael Leslie, 'The Spiritual Husbandry of John Beale', in Leslie and Raylor (eds.), *Culture and Cultivation*, pp. 151–72; James Crossley (ed.), *The Diary and Correspondence of Dr. John Worthington* (2 vols. in 3 parts, Manchester, 1847–86, Chetham Society, vols. 13, 36 & 114), vol. 1, p. 174; British Library, Ms. Evelyn Letters, vols. 1 & 2 (Letters of Beale to Evelyn); British Library, Evelyn Papers Ms. 45 (*Elysium Britannicum*), Hartlib Papers, 28/2/67A, 29/5/54A, 67/22/1A–4B.

17. John Evelyn
Sylva, or a Discourse of Forest-Trees,
and the Propagation of Timber in His Majesties Dominions
London, 1664
fol. in 4s: A–R^4 π^2 A–L^4
235 × 120 mm
Ashm. 1723

Evelyn's *Sylva* was a collaborative work, written at the request of the Commissioners of the Navy, and undertaken by a number of Fellows of the fledgling Royal Society (founded in 1660), following a paper that Evelyn had given to the Society on 15th October, 1662. Perhaps the most successful of the various projects which Evelyn directed on behalf of the Royal Society, *Sylva* was later expanded in its second and third editions, and represented a major part of the Society's claim to have achieved progress in practical matters. It was not a wholly original work, building as it did on the writings of Interregnum improvers like Blith and Austen (see catalogue nos. 15 and 14), who had also been concerned with the danger of a timber famine and with the best means for its remedy.

Among those who contributed to Evelyn's volume was John Beale (1608–83), rector of Yeovil, Somerset, who had been one of Samuel Hartlib's most frequent correspondents during the 1650s. In 1657, Hartlib had published Beale's *Herefordshire Orchards*, which described the cultivation of apple and pear orchards, and extolled the virtues of cider and perry. Beale argued that the planting of orchards would promote trade and industry, without which the word of God was 'at the best ... a pleasant song', and suggested that, in the groves of the orchard, 'we approach the resemblance of Paradise, which God with his own perfect hand had appropriated for the delight of his innocent Master piece' (*Herefordshire Orchards*, pp. 39 & 48). From 1662, Beale had been encouraging the Royal Society to undertake a campaign to promote the growing of cider apples throughout England.

The appendix to Evelyn's discourse of forest trees in *Sylva*, entitled *Pomona*, was largely contributed by Beale, although it was polished and ordered by Evelyn prior to publication. *Pomona* gave advice on the cultivation and management of orchards, and the production of cider. In it, Beale particularly extolled the virtues of redstreak cider, a liquor resembling white wine, and argued for the medicinal benefits of cider consumption. He also defended his choice of fruit for cider making against criticisms raised by Austen. Other Herefordshire cidermen whose writings contributed to *Pomona* included Captain Taylor, whose settling vessel for the drink is illustrated overleaf.

The Garden

Figure 16
A page from John Evelyn's *Sylva, or a Discourse of Forest-Trees*. The text gives instructions for the production of cider and the diagram is of Captain Taylor's design for a settling vessel. *Sylva* was a collaborative work by fellows of the early Royal Society. Information on orchards made up an appendix, entitled *Pomona*, largely contributed by John Beale. Beale particularly extolled the virtues of redstreak cider, a liquor resembling white wine, and argued for the medicinal benefits of its consumption.
Catalogue no. 17, p. 49.

Sylva and *Pomona* continued the debates about the best way to manage forests and orchards for the good of the state and the profit and health of individuals, which had begun in the 1650s. Beale's contributions reflected his belief that real improvement could only come about through a return to ancient practices, of which the oldest was the cultivation of fruit trees in orchards and groves. Evelyn's 'Historical account of the sacredness and use of standing groves', added to later editions of *Sylva*, in 1670 and 1679, to some extent shared Beale's preoccupation with the recreation of Eden in this way, as did Abraham Cowley's poem, 'The Garden', which was printed in the third edition.

Geoffrey Keynes, *John Evelyn: A Study in Bibliophily with a Bibliography of his Writings* (2nd edition, Oxford, 1968), pp. 129-36 & 147-51; J[ohn] B[eale], *Herefordshire Orchards: A Pattern for all England* (London, 1657); Lindsay Sharp, 'Timber, Science and Economic Reform in the Seventeenth Century', *Forestry*, vol. 48 (1975), pp. 51-86; Mayling Stubbs, 'John Beale, Philosophical Gardener of Herefordshire Part II: The Improvement of Agriculture and Trade in the Royal Society (1663-1683)', *Annals of Science*, vol. 46 (1989), pp. 323-363.

18. David Loggan
Oxonia illustrata
Oxford, 1675
fol: 45 double, single, or treble-sheets on guards
352 × 233 mm (engraving illustrated)
Arch. Antiq. A II.13

David Loggan (1635–1700?) was a Danish engraver who came to live at Nuffield, in Oxfordshire, in 1665. There, he set about drawing and engraving views of the city of Oxford and the colleges and halls of the University, some of which he exhibited in 1669, when he was appointed as the University's engraver. By January 1675, the plates for his work were finished, and by June of that year *Oxonia illustrata* had been printed. Loggan's plates complemented the *Historia et antiquitates universitatis Oxoniensis*, written by Anthony Wood, which had been published in the preceding year.

The plate illustrated (overleaf) is number 32 in the volume, Loggan's engraving of Wadham College, dedicated to Dr Giles Strangways. From 1648 to 1659, under the Wardenship of John Wilkins (see catalogue no. 19), Wadham was a focus for natural philosophical debate and enquiry. Clearly visible in this engraving are the tower over the entrance to the College, from which Wilkins' young protégé, Christopher Wren (see catalogue nos. 60 and 65), and others made telescopic observations, and, on the left of the picture, the gardens, which Wilkins enlarged and improved. In the foreground are the trees and groves of the Warden's garden, among which a summerhouse can be made out; in the background is the more formal Fellows' garden, which was laid out on land purchased during Wilkins' Wardenship for a total cost of £72-13-0, and has at its centre a mound, surmounted by a figure of Atlas bearing a globe. Climbing the walls of the Fellows' garden are a variety of fruit trees.

Robert Boyle, who was resident in Oxford for a number of years from 1654, informed Hartlib about the 'peculiar Flowers' to be found growing in Wilkins' garden (*Hartlib Papers*, 29/5/2B [*Ephemerides*, 1655]). Various features of Wilkins' garden intrigued different correspondents of Hartlib. Several were fascinated by the transparent hives, which Wilkins had built to an improved version of William Mewe's design and in which it was possible to observe a cascade of honey. Others commented on the dials and weathercocks which Wilkins had installed, and on his 'watering instrument', a device (based on a design taken from the *Pneumatics* of Hero of Alexandria) with multiple spouts, each in the form of a different figure, which was worked by suction and could generate a mist of water over part of the garden. Evelyn remarked on the 'talking statue' which stood in the garden and was operated by means of a concealed speaking

The Garden

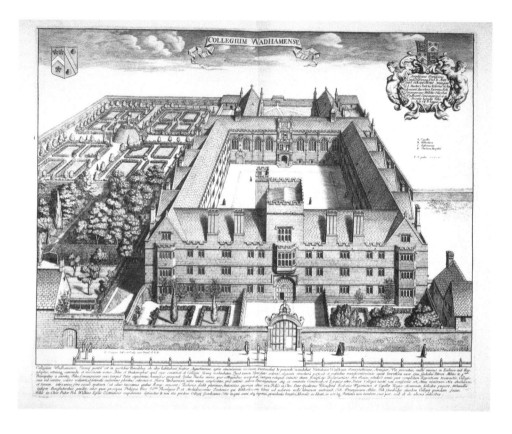

Figure 17

David Loggan's engraving of Wadham College and its gardens, from his *Oxonia illustrata* of 1675. In the 1640s and 1650s, under the Wardenship of John Wilkins, Wadham was a centre for activities relating to natural philosophy. These extended to the garden where, as well as specimens of rare plants, various mechanical curiosities and aids to horticulture were set up. Catalogue no. 18, plate 32.

pipe. Wilkins grew salad crops and Indian wheat in his garden, which was organized, one of Hartlib's correspondents wrote, according to the view that 'what concernes Naturall Philosophy in generall must not be thought Irrelative to Husbandry, which is but an application of it to rural subjects' (Boyle Papers 37). Wilkins' garden was thus a place of improvement and delight, in which learning was harnessed effectively to generate both pleasure and profit.

Falconer Madan, *Oxford Books: a Bibliography of Printed Works Relating to the University and City of Oxford* (3 vols, Oxford, 1895-1931), vol. 3, pp. 304-8; Charles Webster, *The Great Instauration* (London, 1975), pp. 162-3; D. J. Mabberley, 'The Gardens', in C. S. L. Davies and Jane Garnett (eds.), *Wadham College* (Oxford, 1994), pp. 100-21; Royal Society, London, Boyle Papers 37 (Letter to Hartlib, 14th September, 1655); *Hartlib Papers*, 28/1/70A, 29/5/2B, 29/6/19A, 33/1/23A-26B, 70/6/1A-2B.

19. John Wilkins
Mathematicall Magick. Or, the Wonders That May Be Performed by Mechanicall Geometry
London, 1648
8°: A–T⁸ V⁴
142 × 85 mm
Savile H 28

John Wilkins (1614–72) became Warden of Wadham College, Oxford in 1648, following the deprivation of his predecessor by the Parliamentary Visitors. In 1656, he married Cromwell's younger sister, and in 1659 was made Master of Trinity College, Cambridge. Although he had to relinquish that position after the Restoration, he rose rapidly in the Church of England to become Bishop of Chester in 1668. Wilkins was noted for his wide intellectual interests, his skill with the pen, his ability as an organizer, and his moderation in religion. These qualities ensured his success during a period of constant political and religious upheaval in which Wilkins proved himself zealous in defence of the universities and dextrous in negotiations about religious conformity.

Both at Wadham and in London, Wilkins was instrumental in organizing gatherings of individuals with interests in the new natural philosophy. He was closely involved in the foundation and early activities of the Royal Society after 1660, and many of those he had patronized at Oxford subsequently became Fellows of that body. His own reputation was founded on a series of works published in the 1630s and 1640s which discussed discoveries made with new scientific instruments, such as the telescope, and helped to popularize new ideas, like the Copernican system in astronomy. Wilkins was an early enthusiast for the writings of Francis Bacon, and, before he moved to Oxford, had been involved with a group of natural philosophers who met in London from 1645. He had intended to establish a 'Mathematico-Chymico-Mechanical School', and Samuel Hartlib expected him to be appointed president of the standing council of an Agency for the Advancement of Universal Learning which was being canvassed in the late 1640s. Wilkins' interests encompassed a range of Baconian and Comenian themes. These included the reform of education, the invention of a real character and universal language (see catalogue no. 42), agricultural and technological improvement, and religious reconciliation. Like many within the Hartlib circle, Wilkins was a firm believer in the value of knowledge gained from experiment.

Wilkins' interest in technology is most apparent in his book, *Mathematicall Magick*. This work described a number of complex technical devices, and shows that their functioning depended on the operation of a few mechanical laws. It

The Garden

sought to open the way for further technological improvement by demystifying the operations of machines which had previously been kept secret. In places, it was an overly optimistic book, assuming that it would be easy to scale up models into working devices, and underestimating problems caused by friction and other restrictions on the perfect operation of mechanical laws. Such criticisms could certainly be applied to the device illustrated on page 98 of *Mathematicall Magick* (see figure 13, p. 47). This is a system of cogs and a pulley, harnessed to a sail, designed to channel a force as slight as the breath of a human being so that it might lift an oak tree by the roots. Although it was not a practical device, it did serve to illustrate the ways in which brute force could be aided by the operation of pulleys (Evelyn illustrated a not-totally-dissimilar device for uprooting trees in the second edition of his *Sylva*, see catalogue no. 17). Wilkins observed the operation of new agricultural machines near Oxford, and in 1653 had given money to try to establish a repository for scientific instruments and mechanical devices in the University. He also displayed many cunning devices in the Lodgings and gallery at Wadham, where he carried out experiments on perpetual motion.

Much of *Mechanicall Magick* discusses the operation of machines for raising water, such as those which Wilkins had in his garden at Wadham. In general, the book embodied the notion that the quality of human life could easily be improved through the application of experimental knowledge. This was an idea that many linked to the reestablishment of mankind's dominion over nature, which had been lost at the Fall.

Barbara Shapiro, *John Wilkins 1614–1672* (Berkeley and Los Angeles, 1969); Charles Webster, *The Great Instauration* (London, 1975), pp. 88-99, 160-4, & 170-2; *Hartlib Papers*, 62/23/1A-4B, 62/50/5A-6B, 67/11A-B.

20. John Parkinson
Paradisi in sole paradisus terrestris
2nd impression, London, 1656
fol. in 6s: π^2 *^{6} A-3E^6 3F^8
280 × 145 mm
Douce P subt. 42

The punningly-titled 'Park-in-sun's park on earth' was first issued in 1629, and consists of three sections, on flower-gardens, kitchen-gardens, and orchards. Under these headings, it discusses over a thousand plants (of which 780 are illustrated in full-page plates) and their cultivation. John Parkinson (1567-1650) was

The Garden

Figure 18
Portrait of John Parkinson, apothecary to James I and 'Botanicus Regius Primarius' to Charles I. Catalogue no. 20, frontispiece.

well-acquainted with English and Continental botanical and horticultural literature and also drew on the discoveries of a wide circle of fellow botanists and nurserymen in the compilation of his books. An apothecary of Ludgate Hill, Parkinson kept a large and splendid garden at Long Acre where, among other triumphs, he was the first in England to grow the great double yellow Spanish daffodil (in 1618). He was appointed apothecary to James I, and 'Botanicus Regius Primarius' by Charles I. After 1629, he worked extensively on his herbal, *Theatrum botanicum*, published in 1640.

The frontispiece of *Paradisi in sole paradisus terrestris* bears a portrait of Parkinson executed in 1629 (illustrated above). The engraved title-page (see figure 12, p. 42) depicts Adam and Eve dressing the Garden of Eden, and gathering, respectively, fruits and herbs for their food. It shows the Garden bringing forth plenty under God's gaze. In the background, one can make out the mythical Scythian or 'vegetable' lamb, an animal which grew and propagated itself like a plant, and which ate the grass surrounding the single root which anchored it to the earth. This creature was felt by some botanists to provide a link between animals and plants, and was described by Parkinson in his *Theatrum botanicum*. Despite such flights of fancy, which reflected an already out-dated taxonomy, Parkinson's work was considered valuable because of the wide variety of plants which he described and because of his practical experience with them. It is notable for its treatment of salad vegetables, a crop which Evelyn discussed at length in the *Elysium* (catalogue no. 16) and in his *Acetaria* of 1699, where he argued that it had been 'the original, and genuine food of all mankind from the Creation' (*Acetaria*, p. 16). Others regarded fruits as the true first food, and

The Garden

Parkinson's discussion of orchards might be said to look forward also to the work of Austen and Beale (see catalogue nos. 14 and 17).

Simon Manningham, an early owner of this copy, has transcribed Psalm 148: 5 (on creation) and some verses from John Milton's *Paradise Lost* (book IV, lines 623-7, catalogue no. 68):

> To-morrow ere fresh morning streak the east
> With first approach of light, we must be ris'n,
>   And at our pleasant labor, to reform
>   Yon flow'ry arbors, yonder alleys green,
> Our walk at noon, with branches overgrown.

In these lines, Adam speaks to Eve in their bower, at the time of their evening worship, and tells her of their duty to God to dress the Garden of Eden. In the pre-lapsarian world, labour is sweet and easy, since plants grow spontaneously in Eden, and 'mock our scant manuring'. This was the happy state to which many diligent seventeenth-century improvers wished to return the earth, through harder labour and enthusiastic planting and fertilizing.

Blanche Henrey, *British Botanical and Horticultural Literature before 1800* (3 vols, London, 1975), vol. 1, p. 79; R. T. Gunther, *Early British Botanists and their Gardens* (Oxford, 1922), pp. 27 & 265-71; Charles E. Raven, *English Naturalists from Neckham to Ray* (Cambridge, 1947), pp. 248-73; John Prest, *The Garden of Eden* (New Haven, 1981), pp. 7 & 50-1; John Evelyn, *Acetaria. A Discourse of Sallets*, edited by Christopher Driver and Tom Jaine (Totnes, 1996).

21. Jacob Bobart
Catalogus plantarum horti medici Oxoniensis
Oxford, 1648
16° in 8s: A² B⁸-E⁴ A⁸-D²
120 × 70 mm
R. R. z. 269 (1)

In 1621, a gift of £250 from Henry, Lord Danvers (later Earl of Danby) allowed the University of Oxford to take out the lease from Magdalen College of a five-acre tract of meadowland, on a bend of the river Cherwell beyond the East gate of the city, in order to set up a physic garden there. Danvers' gift, together with the benefaction made by Sir Henry Savile to found professorships of geometry and astronomy, promised to transform the teaching of natural philosophy at Oxford. By 1632, the buildings of what is now the University's botanical garden had been erected by Nicholas Stone, a mason who had acted for Inigo Jones, and work had begun to stock it with plants, following the model of earlier physic gardens on the Continent. An attempt to persuade the elder John Tradescant (catalogue nos. 32 and 33) to accept the post of gardener failed in 1637, but, by 1641, Jacob Bobart (*c.* 1596–1680), a native of Brunswick, had been appointed to the post, with a lease on the garden of ninety-nine years, and the right to sell fruit and vegetables from it. Bobart's tasks were 'to dresse manure preserve and keepe the said Garden and from tyme to tyme sett and plant the same with such herbes settes trees and plants as shall be thought requesit and necessarie' (Vines and Druce, p. xvi), for which Danby contracted to pay him £40 a year. Following Danby's death and the sequestration of his lands during the Civil War, Bobart's salary went unpaid for several years, and he lived from the sale of the Physic Garden's produce while the University petitioned Parliament to have his annuity restored. Bobart continued as gardener until his death, and was succeeded in the post by his son, also called Jacob. His care for the Physic Garden won the admiration of many visitors to Oxford, who were impressed by the rare trees and plants which Bobart grew (Evelyn was fascinated by a sensitive plant), by his extraordinary topiary, and, increasingly, by the gardener's own bizarre appearance (see figure 19, p. 66).

In 1648, an anonymous catalogue of the plants to be found in the Oxford Physic Garden was published, containing details of more than 1,600 specimens, of which only about 600 were native to Britain. Many of the plants came from North America. Although the published Latin and English catalogues were the work of unnamed editors (a second edition of 1658 was overseen by Philip Stephens and William Browne), the listings and descriptions of plants were almost certainly Bobart's work. The English preface to the second edition of the catalogue remarked of Bobart's labours in the Physic Garden:

> Thus as the species of all creatures were gathered together into the Arke, comprehended as in an Epitome, so you have the plants of most parts of the world, contained in this garden where they are preserved for thy inspection.

In Bobart's hands, the Physic Garden recreated Eden, in which all the plants of the world had flourished, and provided an example of how hard work and experimental philosophy could restore the fertility of the earth. The garden was also an ark, a refuge from external corruption, and a precursor of a better world to come.

Falconer Madan, *Oxford Books: a Bibliography of Printed Works Relating to the University and City of Oxford* (3 vols, Oxford, 1895–1931), vol. 2, p. 475; Henry Tilleman Bobart, *A Biographical Sketch of Jacob Bobart* ([Leicester], 1884); S. H. Vines and G. Claridge Druce, *An Account of the Morisonian Herbarium* (Oxford, 1914), pp. ix–xxiv; John Newman, 'The Architectural Setting', pp. 135–77 in Nicholas Tyacke (ed.), *The History of the University of Oxford, Volume IV: Seventeenth-Century Oxford* (Oxford, 1997), pp. 169–70.

The Garden

Figure 19
The entrance to the Physic Garden of the University of Oxford. The arch was dedicated to Charles I and to the Earl of Danby, whose gift to the University in 1621 allowed the Garden to be established. Before the entrance stands a figure which can be identified as Jacob Bobart, the first holder of the post of gardener.
Catalogue no. 22, frontispiece.

22. Abel Evans
Vertumnus. An Epistle to Mr. Jacob Bobart, Botany Professor to the University of Oxford, and Keeper of the Physick-Garden
Oxford, 1713
8° in 4s: π² A-D⁴
138 × 85 mm
Gough Oxf. 109 (11)

This poem, which was composed in honour of the younger Jacob Bobart (1641–1719) by Abel Evans of St John's College, contains several references to the elder Bobart. Its frontispiece shows a figure standing before the archway at the entrance to the Physic Garden, which, from its dress, beard and features, can be identified as the elder Bobart, depicted here with a staff and serpent, in the manner of the Greek god of healing, Asclepius.

The Garden

23. Joseph Glanvill
The Vanity of Dogmatizing
London, 1661
8°: A–S⁸
122 × 71mm
Wood 127 (2)

Writing to Samuel Hartlib on 19th April 1661, John Worthington announced:

> There is lately publish'd, The Vanity of Dogmatizing or Confidence in Opinions ... It is a little book in 8vo. The author Jos. Glanville, Master of Arts of Oxford. He is a great valuer of Des-Cartes and Dr. More, whom he often mentions in his book; having been a great reader of his books. He is a young man, and abating some juvenile heat, there are good matters in his book. (*Diary and Correspondence*, vol. 1, p. 300)

Joseph Glanvill (1636–80) studied at Oxford during the 1650s. There he may have met members of the Wadham group of experimental philosophers. Certainly, *The Vanity of Dogmatizing*, which was an attack on scholastic philosophy, drew on the writings of Wilkins as well as those of the Cambridge Platonist, Henry More (1614–87), in its presentation of the virtues of a new natural philosophy. Glanvill was particularly taken by the power of Descartes' sceptical approach to natural philosophy, which he probably learned about initially through More's works. With Hartlib's assistance, More had corresponded with Descartes from 1648. Glanvill was, however, more enthusiastic than More about the possible practical benefits of experimental natural philosophy, and was also influenced by the writings of Bacon (to whose *New Atlantis* he later composed a sequel). Thus, *The Vanity of Dogmatizing* suggested that 'the turning of the now comparatively *desert* world into a *Paradise*, may not improbably be expected from late *Agriculture*' (p. 182).

As well as sharing the conviction of many Interregnum agricultural improvers that the earth could be restored to its pristine fertility, Glanvill believed that advances in philosophy might recreate the perfect knowledge of things which Adam had enjoyed in the Garden of Eden. Then, '*Adam* needed no Spectacles. The acuteness of his natural Opticks (if conjecture may have credit) shew'd him much of the coelestial magnificence and bravery without a *Galilaeo's* tube' (p. 5). Contemporary optical inventions could restore human senses to their original perfection, but the restoration of the Edenic state required human philosophical and spiritual perfectibility also: 'The *Woman* in us, still promotes a deceit, like that begun in the *Garden*; and our *understandings* are wedded to an Eve, as fatal as the *Mother* of our *miseries*' (p. 118). It was this deceit which Glanvill hoped to cure through the practice of a mitigated scepticism.

The Garden

24. Compound Microscope
    English, unsigned, *c.* 1680
    Length of body: 235 mm
    Museum of the History of Science, Inv. no. 42,375

A compound microscope, with a single draw tube, on a tripod stand. The outer pasteboard tube, covered with gold-tooled red leather, slides over an inner one covered with vellum. The lens mounts are lignum vitae; the base is a modern restoration. The microscope is focused by screwing it up and down in the stand. The instrument can be dated by the pattern of decorative tooling.

In the first paragraph of the preface to his book on microscopy, *Micrographia* (catalogue no. 26), Robert Hooke explains the value of optical instruments: 'By the addition of such artificial Instruments and methods, there may be, in some manner, a reparation made for the mischiefs, and imperfection, mankind has drawn upon itself', part of which stems from 'a deriv'd corruption, innate and born with him'. He later explains the source of this inheritance and part of its remedy: 'And as at first, mankind fell by tasting of the forbidden Tree of Knowledge, so we, their Posterity, may be in part restor'd by the same way, not only by beholding and contemplating, but by tasting too those fruits of Natural knowledge, that were never yet forbidden'.

25. Refracting Telescope
    English, unsigned, *c.* 1680
    Length closed: 355 mm
    Museum of the History of Science, Inv. no. 15,115

A five-drawer refracting telescope, the tubes made of pasteboard, covered with vellum, the lens mounts of lignum vitae. The outer tube is decorated with gold tooling.

In explaining the use of a long zenith telescope with a micrometer eyepiece in an attempted measurement of stellar parallax at Gresham College in 1669, Robert Hooke alluded to the contemporary notion of the decline in sensory power since ancient times and drew a humorous parallel with the failing sight of the old: 'Hence I judged that whatever mens eyes were in the younger age of the World, our eyes in this old age of it needed Spectacles; and therefore I resolved to assist my eyes with a very large and good Telescope', (R. Hooke, *Lectiones Cutlerianae* (London, 1679), p. 9).

26. Robert Hooke
Micrographia: Or Some Physiological Descriptions of Minute Bodies Made by Magnifying Glasses
(London 1665)
fol: π² A² a–g² B–C² D–Z⁴ 2A–2K⁴ 2L–2M² (with 38 engraved plates)
220 × 130 mm
Ashmole 1712

Robert Hooke (1635-1703) came up to Christ Church from Westminster School in 1653. By 1655, he was attending meetings of the Oxford group of experimental philosophers. Later, he made experiments on the use of wind power, on springs, and on artificial ways of supplementing the power of human muscles. He explained these to John Wilkins, who gave him a copy of his book, *Mathematicall Magick* (catalogue no. 19), in which such topics were discussed. In the late 1650s, on the recommendation of Thomas Willis, Hooke began to assist Robert Boyle, redesigning the air-pump of Ralph Greatorex, which Boyle subsequently used in his famous experiments on the vacuum. In 1662, Hooke was appointed Curator of Experiments by the newly-founded Royal Society, before whom he was soon required to demonstrate a number of microscopical observations. The findings of these were printed in 1665 as *Micrographia*.

In *Micrographia*, Hooke argued that instruments might help to make up for mankind's loss both of sensory perfection and Adamic knowledge, which was a consequence of the Fall and of original sin. Hooke's plates showed that many things existed in nature which were invisible to the naked eye, and that the microscope could disclose many new appearances. He took the opportunity provided by his examination of the seeds of thyme to rhapsodize on the stupendous variety and beauty to be found among minerals, vegetables, and, above all, animals. He argued that Adam might have been able to name the plants and creatures of the earth (Genesis 2: 19-20) from contemplation (such as that which could now be achieved with the aid of the microscope) of 'the nature, or use, or virtues of bodies, by their several forms and various excellencies and properties' (p. 154). Findings made using new scientific instruments might help to restore what had been lost in Eden, and assist human beings in fulfilling the potential which God had given them: 'And who knows, but the Creator may, in those characters, have written and engraven many of his most mysterious designs and counsels, and given man a capacity, which, assisted with diligence and industry, may be able to read and understand them' (p. 154).

Geoffrey Keynes, *A Bibliography of Dr. Robert Hooke* (Oxford, 1960), pp. 18-23; R. T. Gunther, *Early Science in Oxford* (14 vols, Oxford, 1923-45), vols. 6 & 7, *The Life and Work of Robert Hooke*, vol. 6, pp. 4-10 & 126-220.

The Garden

Figure 20

English compound microscope and refracting telescope, *c.* 1680.
Optical instruments were seen by early Fellows of the Royal Society such as Robert Hooke, and other experimental philosophers, as means of aiding the recovery of an Adamic knowledge of nature.
Catalogue nos. 24 and 25.

The Garden

Figure 21

Plate 18 from Robert Hooke's *Micrographia* – seeds of thyme as viewed with the assistance of a microscope. *Micrographia* was illustrated with many large folding plates of magnified objects, which Hooke used to demonstrate the power of his microscope and its possible role in restoring to contemporary man the perfect sight of Adam, lost at the Fall. From catalogue no. 26.

Figure 22
'And the Lord said unto Noah come thou and all thy house into the Ark'.
The plate is by van Hove and follows Matthaeus Merian's design for the Ark.
Genesis 7: 1. Catalogue no. 5, plate 5, detail.

THE ARK

The story of Noah's Ark has been one of the most appealing and troublesome in the Bible. There is a long tradition in Christian thought of interest in Noah as a type of Christ and in his Ark as an allegory of salvation. The redeemed were preserved in the Ark, which was not so much a ship as a kind of coffin or sarcophagus. They were kept safe from God's righteous anger and delivered to a new life beyond this symbolic death.

As well as its spiritual appeal, the story in itself is charming and compelling. Who could fail to be intrigued by Noah's work of assembling all the animals and housing and caring for his extraordinary menagerie? Who would not tremble at the fate of the cynics and scoffers, locked out of the Ark, their opportunities to repent squandered, as the Flood waters rose around them? Who could not be moved by the helpless craft, shut up for a year and afloat on unknown waters with all life on earth depending on its survival? The popularity of the story of Noah is not surprising.

Problems arose when more rational attitudes and literal interpretations raised new questions about the Ark, but at the same time they gave new significance and importance to Noah. How could an Ark possibly have contained examples of all the animals on earth, not to mention the food they would have needed to eat for a year? What effect would procreation over such a time have had on the viability of the Ark? How could it have rested securely on a mountain top? There were many more problems that demanded attention. Although the questions were numerous, detailed answers were found, and in the process Noah became variously a natural historian, a museum keeper, an astronomer, a shipwright and a navigator.

Noah was a pivotal figure for the intellectual history of mankind just as he was for man's physical survival, and he carried the ancient knowledge of nature that had descended from Adam through his third son Seth to Enoch. Five generations separated Enoch from Seth, but such was the longevity of the patriarchs (Seth died aged 920) that traditions of learning could be constructed between them on the basis of personal knowledge. Adam lived for 930 years, so Enoch knew him. Enoch was generally credited with being the first author and making the earliest written records of the ancient wisdom. Enoch was alive on earth for only 365 years – not because he died, but because 'God took him' – so although Noah was separated from Enoch by only three generations, the chronology in Genesis makes it impossible for him to have known Enoch personally. But he would have known Enoch's son Methuselah, who lived for 967 years (for 243 years of which Adam himself was alive) and there was confidence among Biblical commentators that Noah would have inherited the learning of Enoch, especially since it had been written down.

Adam in his innocence and natural wisdom understood the voice of God, as God communicated with him in the Garden. After the Fall, only two men had that combination of wisdom and righteousness that allowed the record of Genesis to say that they 'walked with God': these two were Enoch and Noah. Little wonder, then, that it was important to extract as much natural knowledge as possible from the building and management of the Ark.

After the Flood, Noah lived to the time of Abraham, so it was not difficult to imagine the authoritative descent extending a few more generations to Moses, the author of Genesis. In connection with both Noah's expertise in astronomy and the writings of Enoch, Walter Ralegh explained things as follows (catalogue no. 30, p. 80):

> ... it is very probable that Noah had seene and might preserve this booke. For it is not likely, that so exquisite knowledge therein (as these men had) was suddenly inuented and found out, but left by Seth to Enoch, and by Enoch to Noah, as hath been said before. And therefore if letters and arts were knowne from the time of Seth to Enoch, and that Noah liued with Methusalem, who liued with Adam, and Abraham liued with Noah, it is not strange (I say) to conceiue how Moses came to the knowledge of the first Age, be it by letters, or by Cabala and Tradition, had the vndoubted word of God neede of any other proofe then self-authoritie.

It is interesting that Ralegh, as historian, argues to substantiate the authority of his primary author, Moses, but then points out that in any case, as scripture, the source has the authority of divine inspiration.

For the students of Noah, God designed the Ark and his servant built it according to the divine blueprint. The Genesis record of God's instructions may be sketchy, but it is clear that measurement and proportion were among God's primary concerns (Genesis 6: 15–16):

> And this is the fashion which thou shalt make it of: The length of the ark shall be three hundred cubits, the breadth of it fifty cubits, and the height of it thirty cubits. A window shalt thou make to the ark, and in a cubit shalt thou finish it above; and the door of the ark shalt thou set in the side thereof; with lower, second, and third stories shalt thou make it.

Apart from this, the material specified was 'gopher wood', there were to be rooms within, while inside and out were to be covered with pitch. From these few details and the people and animals to be accommodated, the commentators worked out their different designs.

The cubit was a fundamental element in these reconstructions and much speculation was devoted to its length and to the consequent size of the Ark. Noah thus became associated with standards of measure, as a practical mathematician and a shipwright. It was generally agreed that the proportions of the Ark, more particularly the ratio of length to breadth, represented those of the human figure, an idea that reinforced the link between the Ark and the Son of Man, that is Christ and his mission of salvation (see catalogue nos. 28 and 37). The most influential image of Noah for natural knowledge was as natural historian and then as museum keeper. To devise a successful Ark required a complete knowledge of the natural world – not only of the species of animals, but their sizes, habits, diets and life cycles. On the basis of this knowledge, the Ark was built as a museum, arranged according to a divine taxonomy, and the effort to ascertain and even to recreate what this might have been had a profound influence on the study of the natural world.

Thus it was important to enumerate all the creatures in the Ark, both to recover Noah's natural history and to solve the problem of finding a design of vessel that would accommodate and sustain them. A further step was to describe them and their conditions of life, to recover the natural knowledge deployed by Noah, and natural histories written along these lines became associated with accounts of the Ark. Finally, it might be possible to emulate Noah himself by collecting and arranging an ark, by assembling and displaying a complete taxonomy of the kingdoms of animals, birds, reptiles, insects and fish. Early museums were often characterized as arks and their keepers as latter-day Noahs (see catalogue nos. 29, 31 to 33, and 37).

27. Jean Buteo
Opera geometrica ... De arca Noe, cuius formæ, capacitatisq; fuerit
Lyons, 1554
4°: a–v⁴
176 × 125 mm
4° B 32 Art. Seld.

The *Opera geometrica* of the French mathematician Jean Buteo was a collection of tracts on a variety of mathematical questions, beginning with the shape and size of the Ark. Buteo was the first to treat this as an exercise in geometry, so to some extent he set the terms of subsequent debate. He considers the materials used in constructing the Ark, the general design, the overall capacity and the accommodation required to cope with all the animals, while central to the discussion is the size of the cubit. Buteo sees no need to invoke the large 'geometrical' cubit for, by limiting the animals to a finite number and by estimating the space they would require, he concludes that they can be accommodated with the necessary provisions. Buteo's calculations were influential because they vindicated a material Ark.

Buteo's technique was to reduce the animal units to three – cow, sheep and wolf – and to express the requirements for accommodation and food in terms of equivalent numbers of these animals. This device makes the whole calculation manageable and he was able to fit his animals into the lowest deck, store the hay in the middle, and leave the top deck for people and birds.

Buteo discusses the variety of forms given to the Ark and establishes the problematic in a graphic manner by presenting five designs of Ark on a single page at the end of a section 'De variis arcæ, & earum scenographia'. The first is attributed to the early Christian scholar Origen, while the second is simply ascribed to 'aliquos doctores'. Buteo's own solution is set at the bottom of the group, and is preceded by designs from the twelfth-century Augustinian scholar Hugh of Saint Victor and from the Dominican general Cajetan or Thomas de Vio. Thus Buteo presents the Ark as a problem of conflicting designs, while at the same time locating it within the discourse of geometry. This rhetorical device, with similar examples, was repeated as late as 1697 by the Dutch shipbuilder Cornelis van Yk.

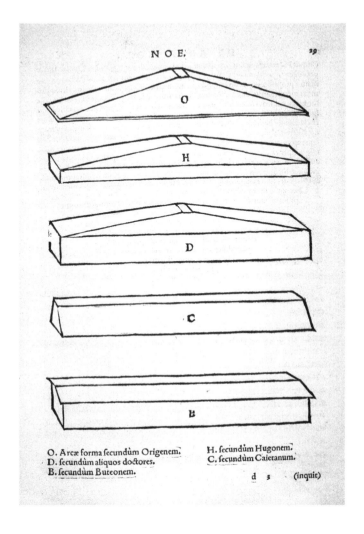

Figure 23
Five possible designs for the Ark, as outlined in Jean Buteo's *De arca Noe*. Buteo's own proposal for the shape of the Ark is at the bottom, labelled 'B', and was widely adopted by later writers. Catalogue no. 27, p. 29.

Just as Buteo's mathematics and its conclusions were widely adopted, so his general design became popular also. It was used, for example, in the illustration included in the Cambridge Bible of 1660, it was adopted by John Wilkins in 1668 and it formed the basis of Kircher's magnificent Ark of 1675.

D. C. Allen, *The Legend of Noah: Renaissance Rationalism in Art, Science and Letters* (Illinois, 1949).

The Ark

28. Benito Arias Montano
Antiquitatum Iudaicarum libri IX
Leiden, 1593
4°: A–2B⁴
202 × 121 mm
AA 66 Th. Seld.

Benito Arias, called Montano (Benedectus Arias Montanus), was a Spanish priest and scholar, who was sent by Philip II to Antwerp to edit the Polyglot Bible of 1572, printed by Plantin. According to Samuel Hartlib, Montano 'was persecuted and imprisoned by the Inquisition for that excellent Work of his of Translating the Bible which tended soe much to the good of Christendome the renowne of the king of Spain and the credit of Popery itself' (*Hartlib Papers*, 28/2/58B [*Ephemerides*, 1653]). Montano was indeed charged with heresy but was acquitted.

Montano's stay in Antwerp had an important influence on his interest in mathematics. Plantin sold instruments and globes from the Louvain workshop associated with Gemma Frisius, particularly globes by Gerard Mercator and mathematical instruments by Gualterius Arsenius. Montano maintained his contact, through Plantin, with the workshop after he had returned to Spain and he arranged the purchase of instruments for Philip's collection.

One of the tracts included in the Antwerp Polyglot was republished as *Antiquitatum Iudaicarum*. Montano devotes more space to the structure and fabric of Solomon's Temple than to Noah's Ark, putting forward a design that came to represent an alternative to that of Villalpando (see catalogue no. 51). However the Temple and the Ark raised similar concerns about geometrical proportions, divine design and sacred measures.

Montano's Ark took the form of a three-storied rectangular box, with one door and window, and a curved roof. He combined the two ideas of the proportions of the Ark being those of a man and the story of the Flood being an allegory of man's redemption, by illustrating the Ark as the coffin of Christ. As a result, the body of Christ, marked with the stigmata, fitted exactly within the proportions of Montano's Ark.

Figure 25 (Far right)
Aldrovandi's elephant as depicted in his natural history of quadrupeds. The *Studio Aldrovandi*, which survives in the collections of the University of Bologna, became the most famous natural history collection of the sixteenth century and its founder was viewed as a 'second Noah'.
In the seventeenth century however, Aldrovani came to be criticized for relying too much on the authority of the ancients – primarily Aristotle and Pliny – as new emphasis was placed on the importance of making observations directly from nature.
Catalogue no. 29, p. 465.

29. Ulisse Aldrovandi
De quadrupedibus solidipedibus volumen integrum
Bologna, 1616
fol. in 6s: π^4 A–2Y^6
282 × 169 mm
A 3.7 Med.

Ulisse Aldrovandi, a professor in the medical faculty of the University of Bologna, created the most famous museum of natural history in the sixteenth century. It was meant to accumulate, organize and display the natural world arranged according to Aristotle and Pliny. As his collection extended and his fame grew, Aldrovandi came to be seen as a second Noah.

His publication programme was incomplete at his death in 1605, but further catalogues appeared in subsequent decades, when responsibility for the *Studio Aldrovandi*, which by 1600 contained about 20,000 items, had been accepted by the Senate of Bologna. The book included in the exhibition, dealing with quadrupeds, was published in Bologna in 1616, and in representing the work of Aldrovandi, must stand for his vast enterprise of collecting, taxonomy, display and publication.

As interest in natural history collections grew in seventeenth-century England, Aldrovandi's approach was revised in favour of a closer scrutiny of actual specimens. Hartlib observed in 1640 that 'Out of all Aldrovandi 10 or 12. Opera scarce one will bee compiled ad rem, i.e. that shall contain a true botanical Historie. The other things bee impertinencys et digressions' (*Hartlib Papers*, 30/4/54B [*Ephemerides*, 1640]). By the time of Grew's catalogue of the Royal Society's collection, published in 1681, a different culture prevailed in natural history (preface, sig. A):

> I have made the Quotations, not to prove things well known, to be true; as one * (and he too deservedly esteemed for his great Diligence and Curiosity) who very formally quotes Aristotle, to prove a Sheep to be amongst the Bisulca ... as if Aristotle, must be brought to prove a Man hath ten Toes.
> *Aldrovandus [printed marginal note]

P. Findlen, *Possessing Nature: Museums, Collecting, and Scientific Culture in Early Modern Italy* (Berkeley, 1994); N. Grew, *Musæum Regalis Societatis* (London, 1681).

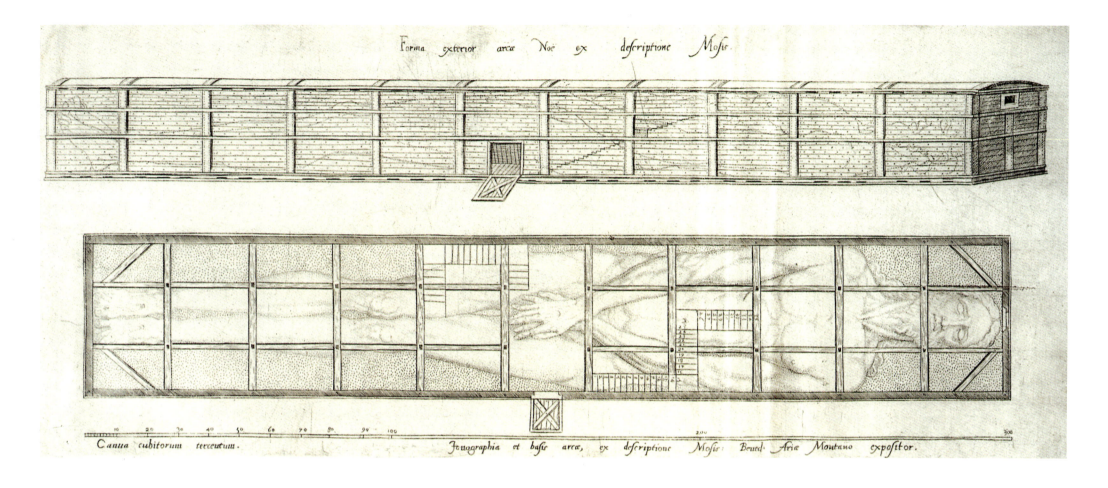

Figure 24
In representing the Ark in his *Antiquitatum Iudaicarum*, Benito Arias Montano chose to combine two ideas: the proportions of the Ark as those of a man, and the story of the Flood as an allegory of man's redemption. In a powerful piece of imagery, he illustrated the Ark as Christ's coffin, with its proportions matching precisely those of Christ's body. Catalogue no. 28, plate facing p. 80.

Montano's Temple (see figure 47) was an influential design, especially for those who were not drawn to the more extravagant elaboration of Villalpando. Philip II appointed Montano as librarian of El Escorial, the monastery-palace whose design was itself related to contemporary reconstructions of the Temple.

K. van Cleempoel *et al.*, *Instrumentos científicos del Siglo XVI: la corte Española y la escuela de Lovaina* (Madrid, 1997); J. A. Ramírez (ed.), *Dios arquitecto: J. B. Villalpando y el templo de Salomón* (Madrid, 1994); and R. Taylor, 'Architecture and Magic: Considerations on the Idea of the Escorial', in D. Fraser, H. Hibbard and M. J. Lewine (eds.), *Essays Presented to Rudolf Wittkower* (2 parts, London, 1967), part 1, pp. 81–109.

29. Ulisse Aldrovandi
De quadrupedibus solidipedibus volumen integrum
Bologna, 1616
fol. in 6s: π⁴ A–2Y⁶
282 × 169 mm
A 3.7 Med.

Ulisse Aldrovandi, a professor in the medical faculty of the University of Bologna, created the most famous museum of natural history in the sixteenth century. It was meant to accumulate, organize and display the natural world arranged according to Aristotle and Pliny. As his collection extended and his fame grew, Aldrovandi came to be seen as a second Noah.

His publication programme was incomplete at his death in 1605, but further catalogues appeared in subsequent decades, when responsibility for the *Studio Aldrovandi*, which by 1600 contained about 20,000 items, had been accepted by the Senate of Bologna. The book included in the exhibition, dealing with quadrupeds, was published in Bologna in 1616, and in representing the work of Aldrovandi, must stand for his vast enterprise of collecting, taxonomy, display and publication.

As interest in natural history collections grew in seventeenth-century England, Aldrovandi's approach was revised in favour of a closer scrutiny of actual specimens. Hartlib observed in 1640 that 'Out of all Aldrovandi 10 or 12. Opera scarce one will bee compiled ad rem, i.e. that shall contain a true botanical Historie. The other things bee impertinencys et digressions' (*Hartlib Papers*, 30/4/54B [*Ephemerides*, 1640]). By the time of Grew's catalogue of the Royal Society's collection, published in 1681, a different culture prevailed in natural history (preface, sig. A):

> I have made the Quotations, not to prove things well known, to be true; as one * (and he too deservedly esteemed for his great Diligence and Curiosity) who very formally quotes Aristotle, to prove a Sheep to be amongst the Bisulca ... as if Aristotle, must be brought to prove a Man hath ten Toes.
> *Aldrovandus [printed marginal note]

P. Findlen, *Possessing Nature: Museums, Collecting, and Scientific Culture in Early Modern Italy* (Berkeley, 1994); N. Grew, *Musæum Regalis Societatis* (London, 1681).

Figure 25 (Far right)
Aldrovandi's elephant as depicted in his natural history of quadrupeds. The *Studio Aldrovandi*, which survives in the collections of the University of Bologna, became the most famous natural history collection of the sixteenth century and its founder was viewed as a 'second Noah'. In the seventeenth century however, Aldrovani came to be criticized for relying too much on the authority of the ancients – primarily Aristotle and Pliny – as new emphasis was placed on the importance of making observations directly from nature. Catalogue no. 29, p. 465.

The Ark

30. Walter Ralegh
The Historie of the World in Five Bookes
London, 1614
fol. in 6s: A–5Z⁶ (a)–(2a)⁶ ☼–2☼⁶ a–b⁶ (with numerous folding plates)
273 × 149 mm
Vet. A2 c. 2

For a writer of history, Noah's Ark was not so much a stimulus to geometry, natural history or biblical exegesis, as a critical episode in the unfolding destiny of man. Thus, one of Ralegh's main concerns is the resting place of the Ark, since it was from here that men and animals re-colonized the earth. He also used the Ark to illustrate several of the themes that animate his concern with the patriarchal age. They relate for the most part to the decline of man and nature. So long as the earth retained something of the vigour of God's creation, the patriarchal life-span was long. Now 'time it selfe (vnder the deathfull shade of whose winges all things decay and wither) hath wasted and worne out that liuely vertue of Nature in Man, and Beasts, and Plants', and we in the old age of the world are reduced to compensating for nature's deficiencies with 'the artificiall helpe of strong waters, hot spices, and prouoking sawces' (p. 77).

But some geometry is inevitably part of the story and Ralegh has an extended taxonomy of cubits, which includes the large 'geometrical' cubit other authors invoked to increase the size of the Ark. This tradition derived from Origen, who held that Moses, since he lived in Egypt, would have used the geometrical cubit of Egyptian measure, which was six times as long as the common one. Ralegh, however, follows Buteo (catalogue no. 27) in his opinion that the common cubit of 18 inches will suffice for the animals Noah had to accommodate. The larger men of the patriarchal age would require, it is true, more space, but since the cubit was the distance from a man's elbow to the tip of his middle finger, the unit of length was also greater 'according to the measure of Giantly stature' (p. 112). Although all of Nature's progeny, including animals, was larger, we can be sure, by applying the golden rule of proportional calculations, that if an ark measured by our reduced and wasted cubit seems sufficient for the decayed state of the natural world, Noah's Ark will have held the men and animals of that more vigorous age: '… it followeth of necessitie, that those large bodies which were in the daies of Noah might haue roome sufficient in the Arke, which was measured by a Cubit of length proportionable' (p. 112).

Ralegh attributed to Noah knowledge of the motions and nature of the heavens, a science passed through Noah's sons to Zoroaster. But he was also remarkably well informed on recent astronomical discoveries, presumably through the agency of Thomas Harriot. Ralegh sought to separate Noah's Flood from the

The Ark

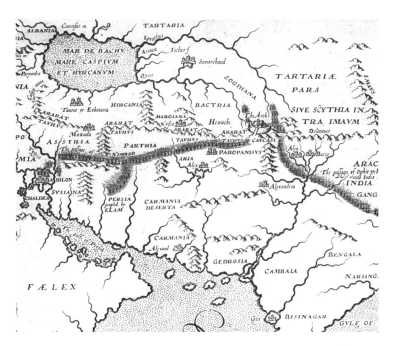

Figure 26

The post-diluvial biblical lands as delineated in Ralegh's *History of the World*, showing the Ark landed on Mount Ararat, a mountain which Ralegh equated with Taurus in the Caucasus (*cf.* Catalogue no. 69). Catalogue no. 30, plate between pp. 108 and 109, detail.

flood 'in the time of Ogyges', and to deny the miraculous nature of the latter. The pagan story of the flood of Ogyges and its relationship to the story of Noah was a problem for biblical commentators, as was that of the later flood of Deucalion, which Deucalion survived with his wife by floating in a large chest. Ralegh adds to this discussion by explaining reported changes in the appearance of Venus. That these were not miraculous portents could be deduced from the observations of Galileo, published in the *Letters on Sunspots* of 1613, the year before Ralegh's *Historie*: 'Galilæus, Galilæus, a worthy Astrologer now liuing, who by the help of perspectiue glasses haue found in the starres many things vnknown to the ancients, affirmeth so much to haue beene discovered in Venus by his late obseruations' (p. 100). Galileo had observed the phases of Venus using a telescope, but an equivalent optical effect might have been produced by the mists and fogs associated with the onset of a flood.

There are many references to Ralegh's *Historie* in Hartlib's *Ephemerides*. At one point Hartlib compares three English literary statesmen, Thomas More, Francis Bacon and Ralegh: 'More was a States-man and divine Verulam a States-man and Philosopher but Raleigh a States-man and a Souldjer. The 2. former the likelier honest-men' (*Hartlib Papers*, 28/1/19B–20A [*Ephemerides*, 1649]).

The Ark

Figure 27 (Opposite)
The interior of the *Museum Wormianum*. Worm's collection was formed in the first half of the seventeenth century. Its lasting fame was ensured by this famous engraving, which depicts a scene that was typical of collections of the period.
Catalogue no. 31, title-page.

31. Ole Worm
Museum Wormianum, seu historia rerum rariorum
Leiden, 1655
fol. in 4s: *⁴ π² A–3C⁴
271 × 152 mm
B 5.9 Art.

The Danish collection of Old Worm is indicative of the growing interest in cabinets of natural history in the seventeenth century and the diffusion of an enthusiasm for collecting from Italy to northern of Europe. Like Aldrovandi, whose work had a profound influence on Worm, the *Museum Wormianum* was formed with a significant professional purpose in mind, namely medical education. Worm was Professor of Medicine at the University of Copenhagen for most of the period in which he was amassing the collection of his museum. But his background had given him the extensive skills required of an ambitious collector: he had travelled widely and had previously held the University chairs of Latin, Greek and natural philosophy.

The museum was arranged according to a hierarchical taxonomy, rising from stones and minerals, through plants and animals to human anatomy and artificial products. This is reflected in the catalogue published in 1655, the year after Worm's death. The collection itself was absorbed into the royal *Kunstkammer*, founded in 1650, but it was Worm's catalogue – particularly its splendid plate of the interior of his museum – that secured his position in the history of the discipline.

O. Impey and A. MacGregor, *The Origins of Museums* (Oxford, 1985).

The Ark

32 & 33. John Tradescant
*Musæum Tradescantianum: or, a Collection of
Rarities Preserved at South-Lambeth Near London*
London, 1656
8°: A⁸ a⁴ B-N⁸
111 × 60 mm
2 copies: Manning 8° 258 and 8° V 90 Art.

The *Musæum Tradescantianum* is the museum that most clearly reflects the popular link between Noah and natural history, for it was generally known as 'The Ark'.

The elder Tradescant was a gardener whose travels in the service of his employers had allowed him to build his collection, and who became Keeper of 'His Majesty's Gardens' in 1630. After his death in 1638, his collection passed to his son, who was also called John and was also a well-travelled gardener, who augmented it and prepared the catalogue. He explained in the preface to the catalogue that he had been persuaded:

> That the enumeration of these Rarities, (being more for variety than any one place known in Europe could afford) would be an honour to our Nation, and a benefit to such ingenious persons as would become further enquirers into the various modes of Natures admirable workes, and the curious Imitators thereof.

Samuel Hartlib was one of those who hoped for a catalogue, noting in 1648 that 'Tradusken should bee induced to make an exact Catalogue of all his Museum' (*Hartlib Papers*, 31/22/32B [*Ephemerides*, 1648]). He was also concerned about attempts to secure its future, either in Oxford or Cambridge.

Tradescant's Ark in Lambeth was open to callers on payment of a fee and became a place of resort for visitors to London. Its contents passed by deed of gift to Elias Ashmole, who made additions from his own collections and presented the whole to the University of Oxford, where it was housed in a building – now the Museum of the History of Science – designed specifically for the purpose and completed in 1683.

A. McGregor (ed.), *Tradescant's Rarities* (Oxford, 1983); O. Impey and A. MacGregor, *The Origins of Museums* (Oxford, 1985).

The Ark

Figure 28
'John Tradescant the elder; who first instituted and enriched the collection of select things and celebrated artifacts in the Lambeth Storehouse near London where they can still be seen.'
Catalogue no. 32, frontispiece.

34. Bladder fish
   Length: 500 mm
   Lent by the University Museum of Natural History

The skin of a bladder fish, *Chilomycterus reticulatus*, thought to have been part of the *Musæum Tradescantianum* in the seventeenth century.

R. T. Gunther, *Early Science in Oxford* (14 vols, Oxford, 1923-45), vol. 3, *Part 2: The Biological Collections*, p. 366.

35. Samuel Bochart
   Hierozoicon, sive bipertitum opus animalibus sacræ scripturæ
   London, 1663
   fol: A–B² a–y² A–4Z⁴ 5A–5H² (vol. 1)
   fol: a–b² B–3K⁴ 3L–4P² (vol. 2)
   298 × 163 mm
   C 3. 10, 11 Th.

Samuel Bochart was a French Protestant pastor at Caen, who combined the interests of a naturalist, a philologist and a theologian, and who acquired an immense reputation as a scholar and authority on ancient languages. He had spent several months studying in Oxford in 1621. His *Geographiæ sacræ* of 1646 (catalogue no. 83) was particularly celebrated and even provoked Queen Christina of Sweden to write to Bochart personally, expressing a desire to meet him. Accordingly, Bochart travelled to Stockholm in 1652 and spent a year in the Swedish court. The manuscripts he found in Stockholm were useful in the preparation of his *Hierozoicon*, and one Arabic manuscript on animals was given to him as a parting gift by Christina.

Geographiæ sacræ contains Bochart's account of the Flood, but it was with his later *Hierozoicon*, first published in London in 1663, that he became a kind of Noah – not in the material sense of Aldrovandi or Kircher, but by deploying philology and biblical exegesis. This enormous work deals with all the animals

Figure 29
Portrait of Samuel Bochart.
Catalogue no. 82.

mentioned in the Bible and their treatment by ancient naturalists, whether Greek, Roman or Arab, while Bochart demonstrates his facility with a formidable range of languages.

Bochart's English biographer Edward H. Smith observed in a short account published in Caen in 1833 that, while he seemed to be little known in France, 'dans ma patrie, au-delà de la Manche, Bochart est vénéré comme un des hommes du plus prodigieux savoir' (Smith, p. 5). Oldenburg had described him to Samuel Hartlib in 1659 as 'the great minister of Caen' (Hall and Boas Hall, p. 330).

A. R. Hall and M. Boas Hall (eds.), *The Correspondence of Henry Oldenburg* (12 vols, 1965–86), vol. 1 (Madison, 1965); E. H. Smith, *Samuel Bochart* (Caen, 1833).

The Ark

36. John Wilkins
An Essay Towards a Real Character and a Philosophical Language
London, 1668
fol. in 4s: π^2 a-d^2 B-3M^4 3a^4 3A-3T^4
235 × 127 mm
Savile A 4

As accounts of the Ark became more elaborate, their natural historical content became more prominent through attempts to name and describe all the animals. In the case of John Wilkins, his 'enumeration and description of the several species of Animals' – a necessary preliminary to a universal language – was the occasion for a consideration of the Ark. He is convinced that 'Philosophy and Mathematicks' can finally defeat the scoffing of sceptics and atheists. These were indeed the two components of contemporary debate: 'philosophy' in this context meant the natural history of animals, while 'mathematicks' referred to the size of the cubit, calculations of the space required and the shape and disposition of the overall design.

In fact Wilkins' treatment of the Ark is, as he acknowledges, a refinement of Buteo's (catalogue no. 27). He establishes an equivalency for each species in terms of one of the three animal units used by Buteo – cow, sheep and wolf – along with space and food requirements for each unit. He is careful to err on the generous side in all cases, providing, for example, 'such fair Stalls or Cabins as may be abundantly sufficient for them in any kind of posture' (p. 165). He calculates that the carnivores will need 1,825 sheep to eat during the year spent in the Ark, but manages to accommodate all the animals required for food along with those preserved for procreation on the lowest of his three stories. This is illustrated above the view of the exterior of the Ark, with the sheep for food in the pens stretching along the middle of the deck. Insects and such small creatures as mice and rats would not require specific accommodation, while snakes, lizards, frogs, and so forth could live happily enough in the bilge. The calculated quantity of hay for the ruminants was easily stored on the middle deck, while Noah and his family lived above with the birds.

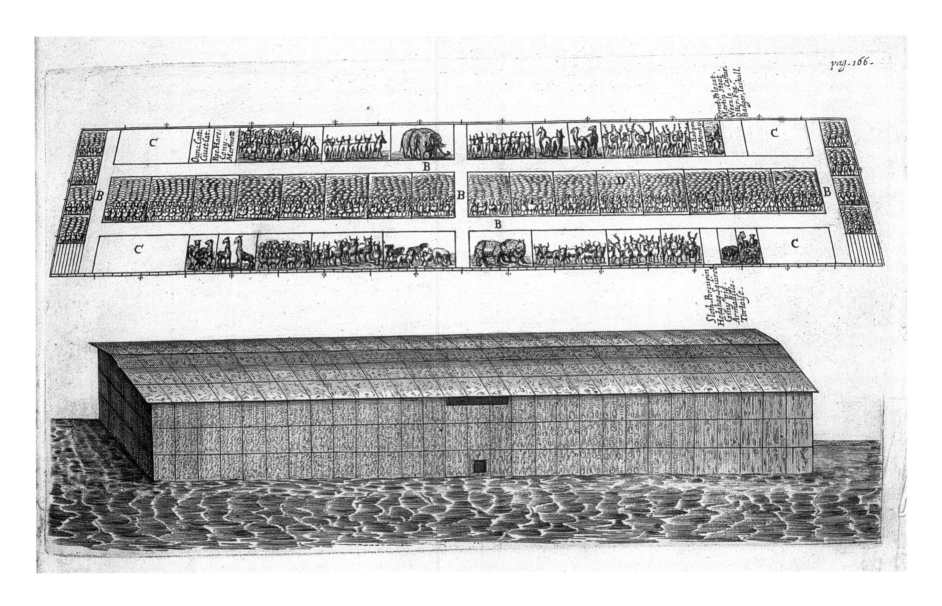

Figure 30

The design of Ark proposed by John Wilkins in his *Essay Towards a Real Character and a Philosophical Language*. Wilkins viewed the Ark not so much as a ship but as a 'Float to swim above water'. He was careful to allow space for enough meat to sustain the carnivores during the year they spent on the waters: 1,825 sheep, illustrated in the engraving packed tightly into pens in the centre of the deck.
Catalogue no. 36, plate facing p. 166.

The design of the Ark, which was not a ship but 'intended only for a kind of Float to swim above water', also followed Buteo, and its dimensions of 300 × 50 × 30 were expressed in the unit of the common cubit. Wilkins addresses the general question of units of length elsewhere in the book, when he observes that the nations of the world are just as divided in this matter as they are in language. His complementary proposal to a universal language is a universal measure based on a natural standard, and the one he favours, which he attributes to Christopher Wren, is the length of a pendulum beating seconds.

The Ark

Figure 31
Kircher's design for the Ark was a three-storied box with a double-pitched roof.
Birds and humans were to reside on the top storey and quadrupeds on the bottom,
with food and water stored in the middle and the serpents left to languish in the bilge.
Catalogue no. 37, plate between pp. 122 and 123.

37. Athanasius Kircher
Arca Noë, in tres libros digesta
Amsterdam, 1675
fol. in 4s: *–2*^{4} A–2I^4
282 × 155 mm
C 4. 5 Jur.

The most famous and elaborate account of the Ark produced in the seventeenth century was by the Jesuit polymath of the *Collegio Romano*, Athanasius Kircher. Not only was he concerned to reconstruct the story of the Ark in every detail, but he came to personify the impulse for collecting natural history – given sacred purpose through Noah – as he brought together and accommodated the extraordinary *Museum Kircherianum* in Rome. The connection was evident for Kircher: he described Noah's Ark as the first museum.

For Kircher the authority of the Ark as a blueprint derives from its divine origin: unlike other memorable creations of the ancient world, such as the pyramids of Memphis, the walls of Babylon, the statue of Jupiter at Olympus or the Temple of Diana at Ephesus, the Ark was designed by God. Since God was the architect, the design embodies the divine laws of symmetry and proportion, qualities the Ark shares with the Tabernacle of Moses and the Temple of Solomon.

But God also made man, and in his own image. Thus the proportions of man are reflected in the Ark. The length of 300 cubits to the width of 50, for example, is in the same proportion as the height of a well-proportioned man to his width. Such relationships are illustrated by Kircher's diagram, 'Proportio humani corporis ad Arcam comparata'.

As for the shape of the Ark, Kircher says this is controversial, and he relates some of the conclusions of other commentators. His proposal, which had benefited from experimental reconstructions of scale models, is a three-storied box with a double-pitched roof. Kircher owes much to Buteo (catalogue no. 27), but every aspect is elaborated into a detailed description supported by an engaging narrative. In one dramatic illustration of the progress of the Flood, the general arrangement of the scene and the disposition of the condemned people are clearly related to those in the ceiling of the Sistine Chapel, as Kircher would have known it in Rome, but he has replaced Michaelangelo's Ark with his own design.

Kircher comes into his own when enumerating, describing and illustrating the animals. Just as Noah had learnt the science of geometrical proportion from

The Ark

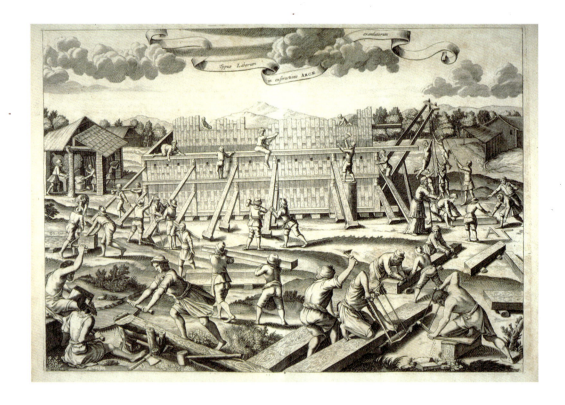

God, so had he also learnt the divine science of animals. Organization and taxonomy were critical to the management of a successful Ark, which had to be divided up into quarters proper for all the animals and their provisions. This Kircher does with obsessive thoroughness and loving detail. Birds and humans were on the top storey, quadrupeds on the bottom, and food and water stored in the middle. Serpents were left to languish in the bilge, while there was no need to provide space for creatures that generated spontaneously, such as the insects and frogs.

A further natural philosophical aspect of the story of Noah's Ark, more evident in Kircher's account than in earlier ones, is the set of meteorological, cosmological and perhaps astrological issues surrounding the phenomenon of the Flood – issues that come together in the discipline later named by Thomas Burnet the 'Theory of the Earth'. Kircher's interest in the subterranean world gave him a rich resource for speculation on the origins of the diluvial water.

After the Flood, Noah lived a further 350 years and died at the age of 950, and Kircher continues his story to the end. He himself had only five years after the

Figure 32 (Left)
Noah directs the building of the Ark.
Catalogue no. 37, plate between pp. 28 and 29.

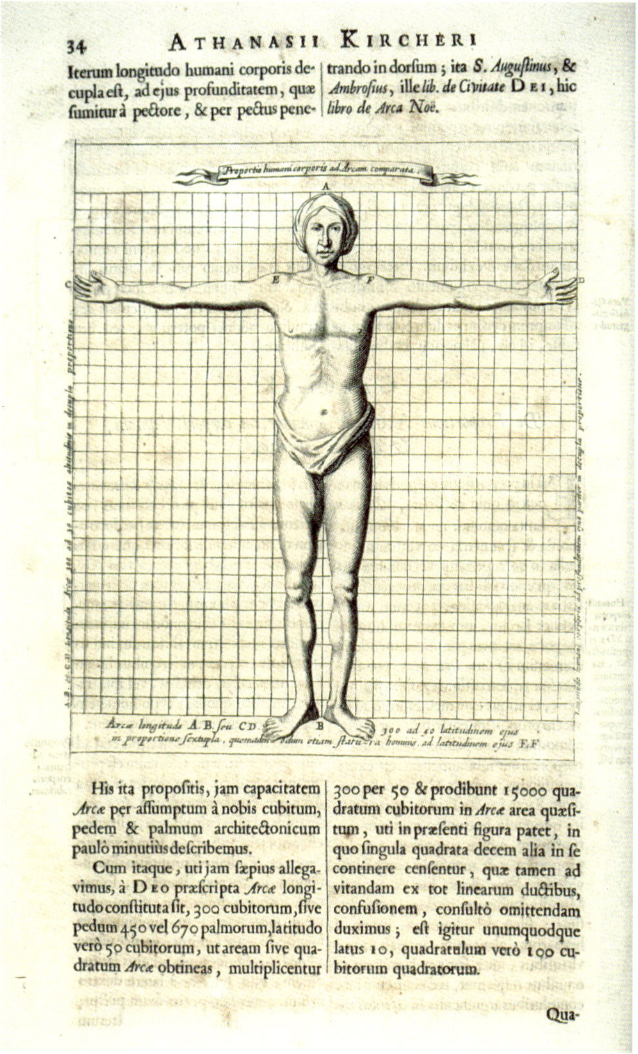

Figure 33 (Right)
Kircher's illustration showing the proportions of the Ark compared to those of man: the ratio of the length of the Ark to its width is 6 to 1, the same as the ratio between the height of a man and the span of his shoulders.
Catalogue no. 37, p. 34.

publication of *Arca Noë* to pursue his mission to recover and display Noah's divine science in his museum in Rome.

D. C. Allen, *The Legend of Noah: Renaissance Rationalism in Art, Science and Letters* (Illinois, 1949); P. Findlen, *Possessing Nature: Museums, Collecting, and Scientific Culture in Early Modern Italy* (Berkeley, 1994); J. Godwin, *Athanasius Kircher. A Renaissance Man and the Quest for Lost Knowledge* (London, 1979); R.W. Unger, *The Art of Medieval Technology: Images of Noah as Shipbuilder* (New Brunswick, 1991).

The Ark

Figure 35 (Right)
John Wilkins' calculation of the number of the different types of beast in the Ark, together with the space that they would require. As the table shows, Noah took seven of every 'clean' and two of every 'unclean' beast. Catalogue no. 36, p. 164.

Figure 34 (Left)
Portrait of John Wilkins. Catalogue no. 38.

38. Portrait of John Wilkins
    By Mary Beale
    Oil on canvas
    1240 × 1000 mm
    Lane Poole no. 141

Wilkins is represented by catalogue nos. 19, 36 and 43.

R. Lane Poole, *Catalogue of Portraits in the Possession of the University, Colleges, City, and County of Oxford* (3 vols, Oxford, 1912–26), vol. 1, p. 57.

For the more distinct clearing up of this, I shall first lay down several tables of the divers species of beasts that were to be received into the Ark, according to the different kinds of food, wherewith they are usually nourished, conteining both the number appointed for each of them, namely, the clean by sevens, and the unclean by pairs, together with a conjecture (for the greater facility of the calculation) what proportion each of them may bear, either to a Beef, or a Sheep, or a Wolf; and then what kind of room may be allotted to the making of sufficient Stalls for their reception.

Beasts feeding on Hay.			Beasts feeding on Fruits, Roots and Insects.			Carnivorous Beasts		
Number.	Name.	Proportion to Beeves.	Breadth of Stalls. feet	Number.	Name.	Proportion to Sheep.	Breadth of the Stalls. feet	Number.	Name.	Proportion to Wolves.	Breadth of their Stalls. feet
2	Horse	3	20	2	Hog	4		2	Lion	4	10
2	Asse	2	12	2	Baboon	2		2	Beare	4	10
2	Camel	4	20	2	Ape	2		2	Tigre	3	8
2	Elephant	8	36	2	Monky			2	Pard	3	8
7	Bull	7	40	2	Sloth			2	Ounce	2	6
7	Urus	7	40	2	Porcupine	7	20	2	Cat	2	6
7	Bisons	7	40	2	Hedghog			2	Civet-cat		
7	Bonasus	7	40	2	Squirril			2	Ferret		
7	Buffalo	7	40	2	Ginny pig			2	Polecat		
7	Sheep	1		2	Ant-bear	2		2	Martin		
7	Stepciseros	1	30	2	Armadilla	2		2	Stoat	3	6
7	Broad-tail	1		2	Tortoise	2		2	Weesle		
7	Goat	1				—	—	2	Castor		
7	Stone-buck	1	30			21	20	2	Otter		
7	Shamois	1						2	Dog	2	6
7	Antilope	1						2	Wolf	2	6
7	Elke	7	30					2	Fox		
7	Hart	4	30					2	Badger	2	6
7	Buck	3	20					2	Jackall		
7	Rein-deer	3	20					2	Caraguya		
7	Roe	2	36								
2	Rhinocerot	8									
2	Camelopard	6	30								
2	Hare		2 Sheep								
2	Rabbet										
2	Marmotto										
		92	514							27	72

In this enumeration I do not mention the Mule, because 'tis a mungrel production, and not to be rekoned as a distinct species. And tho it be most probable, that the several varieties of Beeves, namely that which is stiled *Urus, Bisons, Bonasus* and *Buffalo*, and those other varieties reckon-
ed

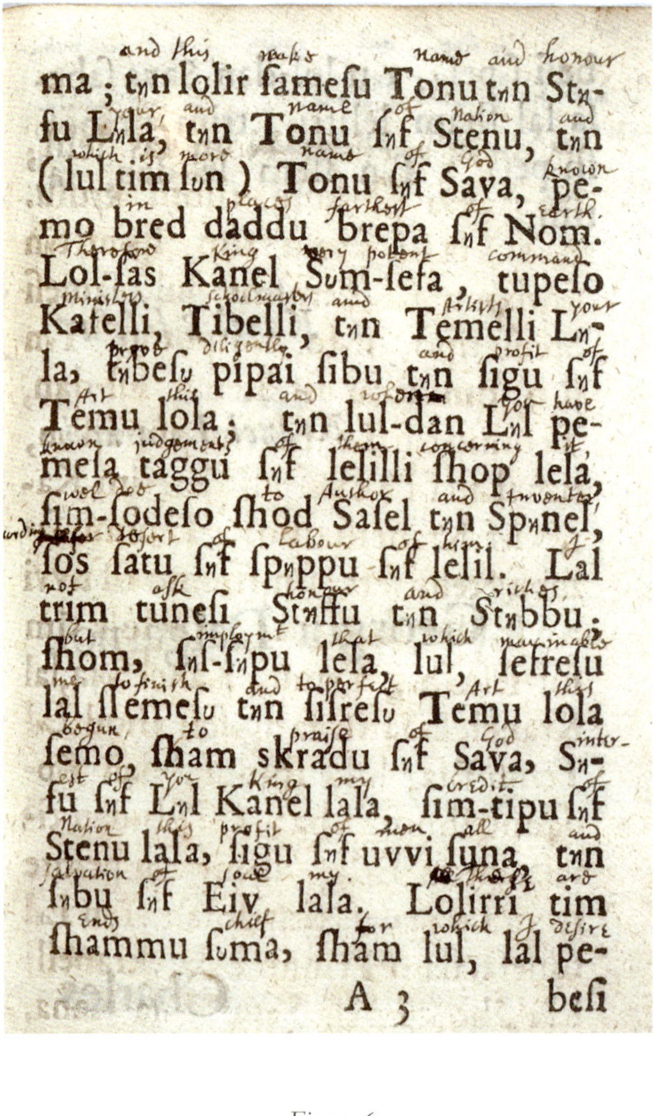
ma; tηn lolir ſameſu Tonu tηn Stη-
ſu Lηla, tηn Tonu ſηf Stenu, tηn
(lul tim ſυn) Tonu ſηf Sava, pe-
mo bred daddu brepa ſηf Nom.
Lol-ſas Kanel Sυm-ſeſa, tupeſo
Kaſelli, Tibelli, tηn Temelli Lηla, tηbeſυ pipai ſibu tηn ſigu ſηf
Temu lola: tηn lul-dan Lηl pe-
mela taggu ſηf lelilli ſhop lela,
ſim-ſodeſo ſhod Saſel tηn Spηnel,
ſos ſatu ſηf ſpηppu ſηf lelil. Lal
trim tuneſi Stηffu tηn Stηbbu.
ſhom, ſηſ-ſηpu leſa, lul, ſefreſu
lal ſſemeſυ tηn ſiſreſυ Temu lola
ſemo, ſham skradu ſηf Sava, Sη-
fu ſηf Lηl Kanel lala, ſim-tipu ſηf
Stenu lala, ſigu ſηf uvvi ſuna, tηn
ſηbu ſηf Eiv lala. Lolirri tim
ſhammu ſυma, ſham lul, lal pe-
A 3 beſi

Figure 36

The dedication from George Dalgarno's *Ars signorum*, written in his proposal for a 'universal language'. An English gloss has been added. Catalogue no. 42, sig. A3 recto.

THE TOWER

Chapters 10 and 11 of Genesis contained material which was interpreted by seventeenth-century commentators as providing an account of how the world was peopled after the Flood. Chapter 10 revealed detailed genealogical information about the descendants of Noah and his sons, while chapter 11 related the story of the Tower of Babel, in which God had punished the vain pride of humans (demonstrated by their attempt to build a tower to reach the sky) by laying upon them the confusion of tongues, which resulted in their dispersion geographically and into ethnic groups.

The genealogical details provided in Genesis 10 gave scant geographical evidence with which to identify the locations where the descendants of Noah had lived, but, by combining the suggestions made in Genesis with etymological suppositions about the origins of the names of races mentioned subsequently in the Bible, early modern critics were able to supply a history for most of the peoples of the Middle East. Theological assumptions encouraged them to be more ambitious than this. They believed that God had intended the whole world to be populated, and that he had divided it between the offspring of Noah's three sons (Genesis 9: 25-7 and 10: 32). Thus they searched for linguistic or historical evidence to prove the descent of all nations from the sons of Noah. They derived names to be found in classical and oriental history and literature from biblical originals, often demonstrating great erudition and considerable imagination in the course of arguments that never proved less than contentious.

Although individual conclusions often differed markedly from one another, there was general consensus on both the assumptions and the methods necessary for the construction of biblical and universal history. There was also widespread agreement on the necessity of the task, and its usefulness for a proper understanding of the Bible and its prophecies. Nevertheless the sources for such historical projects remained uncertain, with many authors relying on materials (such as the pseudo-Berossos) which were effectively the products of Renaissance forgery. Debate could therefore be violent, and, despite the local success of works like Ralegh's *Historie* (catalogue no. 30), no one view of biblical or universal history ever succeeded in establishing intellectual hegemony. Far from detracting from the historical importance which was placed on the Bible as a source, however, this failure threw scholars back on scriptural material and on a search for alternative kinds of evidence (such as that of archaeology) with which to confirm it.

The mechanism by which God had ensured the dispersion of peoples across the globe was the confusion of their language. The story of the building of the Tower of Babel provoked a variety of responses during the seventeenth century. For many political thinkers, the tyrannical decision to build the Tower (which was normally ascribed to Nimrod, who was held to be in rebellion against the rightful authority of Noah) represented a defining moment in the history of government. To others, the political meaning of the story was less essential than its implications for human knowledge, language, and ethnography. Prior to the building of Babel, human beings had all belonged to one family, and had spoken one language, which preserved elements of the true language that Adam had used in Eden (identified with Hebrew by many authors). After the confusion of tongues, languages had decayed and multiplied by natural as well as providential means, causing divisions among people. Nations had been formed, and humanity had been dispersed across the globe.

During the sixteenth and seventeenth centuries, a number of authors attempted to establish the history of the development of language since Babel, often in order to trace the spread of peoples, in particular across Europe. They sought to use linguistic material to differentiate the history of the various races within Europe. Others were principally concerned with the understanding of oriental languages and were frequently beguiled by the biblical story of Babel into making too simplistic an analysis of their similarities and differences. Thus, Christian Ravis argued for the integrity of the Semitic languages, tending to view them as little more than dialects of Hebrew (see catalogue no. 78). Although he developed a more relativistic view of the importance of Hebrew, Brian Walton (see catalogue nos. 73, 75 and 77) even continued falsely to incorporate Persian and Armenian with it in the same family of languages.

Much linguistic scholarship was devoted to establishing the text of the Bible and understanding the languages in which it had been written. However, its conclusions also had implications for the history of knowledge. In particular, humanist ideas of *copia* (abundance or richness) were deployed to support the notion that Hebrew might have been the original language. With other oriental languages, it was taken to have a simple economy of vocabulary and expression which could contain all the meanings of the more extensive European languages in a smaller compass. This was held to indicate its rhetorical sophistication and primitive purity. In Hebrew and other Semitic languages, the division between words (or at least roots) and the things which they represented was supposedly less extreme than in the more developed (or decayed) western tongues.

The desire to surmount the arbitrary division between words and things lay behind much seventeenth-century work on the idea of a universal language. Inspired by the writings of Bacon (catalogue no. 53) and Comenius (catalogue nos. 39 and 40), several authors, including a number of members of the Hartlib circle, tried to overcome the curse of linguistic division in this way. They hoped to promote trade, missionary work, and international harmony by establishing an agreed means of communication. Beyond these aims lay the goal of a real, scientific language which might recover for humanity the ability to express concisely the true knowledge of things that Adam had once enjoyed before the Fall. The decay to which all contemporary human tongues were naturally prey, resulting from the curse laid on them at Babel, which many assumed to have afflicted even Hebrew as it survived in the modern world, prompted reformers to seek to create an artificial language rather than to try to re-establish Adam's speech by philological means. This work ideally required the collection and analysis of a huge amount of information about the natural world in order to classify it accurately and establish the structures which would make up the new universal language. The work of John Wilkins (catalogue no. 43) and his collaborators came closest to achieving this impossible task. It demonstrated that the historical curse of Babel could be a spur to considerable natural philosophical endeavour in the seventeenth century and could encourage people to reshape the parameters of their knowledge. This was also the task of education in the thinking of Hartlib and his circle. For them, a true understanding of the world could only be achieved if people had been taught to reason correctly, and to analyse information (especially the experience of their senses) in a useful way. They sought to purge educational and philosophical practice of the errors which Bacon had identified in them, mainly through the adoption of the reformed methods of teaching advocated by Comenius.

Comenius's educational ideas had developed out of the scholastic and encyclopaedic traditions of the new central European Protestant universities. Although they were traditional in some respects, they represented a considerable departure from standard Aristotelian thinking about the world and from the way in which such knowledge had usually been imparted. Hartlib hoped that it would be possible to reform school and university education in England and made a number of attempts to put his ideas into practice. It was unfortunate that other, less thoughtful, but more socially radical critiques of English education were published at much the same time as some of his schemes. In the end, traditional methods, and certainly traditional institutions, came through the period of the Civil Wars and Interregnum relatively unscathed. This was partly because they proved far more adaptable than their critics allowed, but also because state support was usually lacking for anything more adventurous than ensuring the political conformity of the universities of Oxford and Cambridge.

The Tower of Babel was, like the Garden of Eden, in part a reminder of the failures imposed by human pride. But the events which had taken place at Babel, like those which had happened in the Garden, were also crucial for the development of the providential course of history. Without them, human beings might have resisted the divine command to people the earth (Genesis 1: 28). The second part of that instruction promised that human beings would eventually establish mastery over nature, a prophecy which Samuel Hartlib and his contemporaries hoped to see fulfilled in their own times. As well as being a monument to the fallen state of human knowledge, the Tower was therefore a tantalizing symbol of what might be preserved and achieved if people were able to co-operate with God's plans.

Daniel Droixhe, *La linguistique et l'appel de l'histoire (1600−1800): Rationalisme et révolutions primitivistes* (Geneva, 1978); Alain Schnapp, *La conquête du passé: Aux origines de l'archéologie* (Paris, 1993); Terence Cave, *The Cornucopian Text* (Oxford, 1979).

Figure 37
Engraved portrait of Jan Amos Komenský, known as Comenius. Comenius developed a Christian philosophy, or *pansophia*, which sought to harmonize the senses, reason, and scripture, and part of which was to be a universal, philosophical language that would ease communication and understanding. Catalogue no. 39, frontispiece.

39. John Amos Comenius
Janua linguarum reserata: The Gate of Languages Unlocked
translated by Thomas Horne, revised by John Robotham and 'W. D.'
8th edition, London, 1650
8°: π¹ A–2C⁸ 2D²
145 × 90 mm
Mason AA 287(2)

Comenius's *Janua linguarum* was one of the most successful pedagogical works of the seventeenth century. Initially published in 1631, it was soon translated into a number of European languages, and quickly came to the attention of Samuel Hartlib, who began a correspondence with Comenius in 1632, and published several of his works. Hartlib was unable to obtain the profits of John Anchoran's English-Latin-French edition of 1633 for Comenius, but was more closely involved in the bilingual English-Latin edition of Thomas Horne (1610–54), published in 1636. Horne's translation was revised by John Robotham and by 'W. D.', whom Anthony Wood identified as William Dugard (*Athenae Oxonienses*, vol. 2, p. 106), and went through a total of ten editions by 1659.

Originally intended as a first reader, for teaching Latin and the vernacular, the *Janua linguarum* evolved into a thesaurus, many parts of which were devoted to practical information about daily life and the natural world. It was structured into one hundred chapters, each on a different theme, originally made up of one thousand sentences which drew on about eight thousand of the most common Latin words. As it expanded, the linguistic content of the *Janua linguarum* became more complex, but its careful philosophical structure was preserved. This began with the creation of the four elements, and the nature of the earth, plants and animals, and moved on to human anatomy and physiology before discussing rustic and mechanical arts, philosophy, civil society, and, finally, religion and divine providence.

Jan Amos Komenský (1592–1670), known as Comenius, was a bishop of the Czech Unity of Brethren. With his fellow Protestants, he was exiled from Bohemia in 1628, and became a master, and later rector, at the gymnasium of Leszno, in Poland. He developed a Christian philosophy, or *pansophia*, which sought to harmonize the senses, reason, and scripture. His writings contain strong elements of neoplatonism, as well as a faith in inductive reasoning and empirical knowledge which appealed to English Baconians. Works like the *Janua linguarum* also betray the influence of his mentor, the encyclopaedist Johann Heinrich Alsted.

Hartlib enticed Comenius to England in the autumn of 1641, at a time when it seemed possible that there might still be a peaceful reformation of church and state. Whilst in London, Comenius worked on his chiliastic *Via Lucis* (eventually published in 1668), which described, among other things, the work of a Universal College in the perfection of religion and learning and the promotion of the welfare of mankind. The tools with which this College would equip people included 'new schemes for the better cultivation of all languages, and for rendering a polyglot speech more accessible, and finally for establishing a language absolutely new, absolutely easy, absolutely rational, in brief a Pansophic language, the universal carrier of Light' (*The Way of Light*, p. 8).

Comenius planned a philosophical language which would be universal, to ease communication and understanding, much as his philosophically-grounded system for teaching in the *Janua linguarum* had aided the acquisition of tongues. To further Comenius's work, Hartlib published the heads of his programme of educational reform in *A Reformation of Schooles* (1642), for whose frontispiece the engraved portrait of Comenius illustrated in figure 37 was cut. However, later in 1642, Comenius was tempted by Louis de Geer to abandon England for Sweden, leaving Hartlib and his friends to work on alone.

Comenius's work promised to overcome the curse of Babel by re-founding human language on a reformed philosophy, basing it on a simplified range of concepts which reflected a rational analysis of the natural world. The essence of these ideas can be detected in the form of the *Janua linguarum*, the book which made Comenius's reputation as a teacher and philosopher.

Charles Webster (ed.), *Samuel Hartlib and the Advancement of Learning* (Cambridge, 1970), pp. 22–38 & 208; Charles Webster, *The Great Instauration* (London, 1975), pp. 108–110; G. H. Turnbull, *Hartlib, Dury and Comenius* (Liverpool, 1947), pp. 342–464; M. W. Keatinge (ed.), *The Great Didactic of Jan Amos Comenius* (London, 1896), pp. iii & 18–48; Dagmar Čapková, 'Comenius and his Ideals: Escape from the Labyrinth', in Mark Greengrass, Michael Leslie, and Timothy Raylor (eds.), *Samuel Hartlib and Universal Reformation* (Cambridge, 1994), pp. 75–91; Jana Přívratská and Vladimír Přívratský, 'Language as the Product and Mediator of Knowledge: The Concept of J. A. Comenius', in Greengrass, Leslie, and Raylor (eds.), *op. cit.*, pp. 162–73; Robert Fitzgibbon Young, *Comenius in England* (Oxford, 1932); John Amos Comenius, *The Way of Light*, translated by E. T. Campagnac (Liverpool, 1938); Anthony Wood, *Athenae Oxonienses* (2 vols, London, 1691–92).

40. John Amos Comenius, translated by Charles Hoole
Orbis sensualium pictus
3rd edition, London, 1672
8°: A–X^8
125 × 80 mm
Lister I 44

During the 1650s, Comenius composed several books which might serve as introductions to the *Janua linguarum*. The most successful of these was the *Orbis pictus*, which made explicit the Comenian belief that true philosophy should be grounded on a real, empirical language (that is, in a knowledge of things not of words). One of the consequences of the confusion of tongues at Babel had been the loss of the true, original language of mankind, in which there had been a direct correspondence between words and the things that they named. This had been the language that Adam had used to name the beasts in Eden (Genesis 2: 19–20, quoted in English and Latin on the verso of the title-page of *Orbis pictus*). Following in the steps of a number of other teachers, Comenius sought to exploit the immediate connection made between a picture and the thing it represents in order to assist the teaching of reading in Latin and the

The Tower

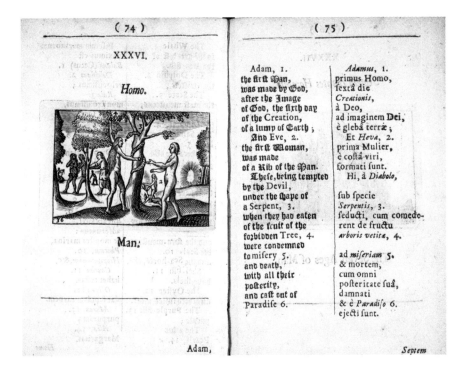

Figure 38

An opening from Comenius's *Orbis sensualium pictus* illustrating his method for teaching languages by exploiting immediate connections between words and pictures. Catalogue no. 40, pp. 74–75.

vernacular. Thus, the *Orbis pictus* consisted of some 150 pictures, each containing several numbered objects which corresponded to numbered words and phrases printed on the facing page. As in the *Janua linguarum*, the order of the pictures, and of the presentation of words and phrases, was a philosophical one, beginning with God and the creation of the elements, and moving on through plants and animals to human beings, and thence to human activities, from farming through the various mechanical arts to social behaviour, ending with philosophical concepts and the doctrines of religion.

The technique of *Orbis pictus* can be seen in the pages illustrated above. These begin the section of the book discussing human beings, which moves on to topics such as the seven ages of man, human anatomy and physiology, and the nature of the human soul, before discussing human inventions in a perceived chronological order (starting with gardening and agriculture). The introduction of human beings into the book is also given a historical context, since the picture (which is clearly based on contemporary illustrations for the Bible – see catalogue nos. 6 and 8) refers to events described in the book of Genesis. The historical nature of the creation of man and woman is mentioned, and the events of the Fall are narrated in words and in the picture. *Orbis pictus* was itself a work of Comenian *pansophia*; it was rationally ordered, and communicated through the senses knowledge which was derived from both the book of scripture and that of nature.

Orbis pictus was first published with a Latin and German text in Nuremberg in 1658, with woodcut illustrations by Paul Kreutzberger. It was translated into English almost immediately by Charles Hoole (1609-67), a former master at Rotherham Grammar School who kept a private school at Lothbury in London. Hoole's translation of 1659 showed a number of changes to Comenius's original, in particular the use of copper plates for the engravings. It was reprinted several times during the seventeenth century, although, from 1672, the quality of the printing of the pictures, in particular, declined. Hoole was principally concerned with the practical problem of teaching Latin to very young children. Thus, his edition of the *Orbis pictus* did not always make explicit the idea of teaching through sense experience which was so essential to Comenius, and about which Samuel Hartlib had been enthusiastic (Turnbull, p. 65):

> The examination of those sensual objects with a plain and most familiar description of them doth properly belong for the direction of it to such bookes as Mr. Com(enius) cals Schola Materna Infantiae etc.; I long extreamly to see how hee hath handled this doctrine of the senses, which is so fundamentally requisite for all his other superstructions.

John Amos Comenius, *Orbis Pictus*, edited by John E. Sadler (London, 1968), pp. 58-80 & 436-41; G. H. Turnbull, *Hartlib, Dury and Comenius* (Liverpool, 1947), pp. 65 & 359-60.

41. Francis Lodwick
A Common Writing
[London], 1647
4°: A-E⁴
154 × 98 mm
Vet. A3 e. 350

During the 1640s and 1650s, several authors based in England attempted to produce universal, real or philosophical characters and universal languages. A number of stimuli may have provoked them to this activity. Francis Bacon had already suggested the need for a philosophical writing in which there was a direct correspondence between words and things, and the idea of a universal character, as a means of communication, had been taken up by John Wilkins in his *Mercury* of 1641. Comenius and others had argued for the usefulness of a universal language, based on a reformed philosophy and on the natural ordering of things. Others were concerned about improving the speed or security of communications and overcoming the expensive barriers posed by differences between vernaculars, or wished to make it easier for children to learn how to communicate.

Advances in shorthand writing from the late sixteenth century, and in cryptography, especially during the Civil Wars, as well as the discovery of new kinds of human language and writing, such as Chinese, helped to encourage people to believe that breakthroughs could be made in these areas. Behind much linguistic work lay the conviction that human beings had once all spoken the same language, and that, before the Fall, Adam had named things using a language which corresponded exactly to nature. What had once come naturally to human beings might now be restored through diligence and effort, not least because a universal language would prove to be a providential tool for spreading the Gospel to newly-discovered lands, such as America. As Robert Boyle wrote to Samuel Hartlib, 'If the design of *the Real Character* take effect, it will in good part make amends to mankind for what their pride lost them at the tower of *Babel*' (Letter dated 19th March 1647, in *Works of the Honourable Robert Boyle*, vol. 1, p. xxxvii).

Francis Lodwick (1619–94), a merchant from the refugee community which worshipped at the Dutch church of Austin Friars in London, was the first person to publish a design for a universal character (the *Common Writing*) and for a universal language (*The Ground-Work or Foundation Laid for the Framing of a New Perfect Language*, in 1652). His *Common Writing* was based on a grammatical analysis of language, which led to the development of a series of symbols or augmentations, each of which would modify a root word or character in the same way. These symbols (mostly additional strokes or points) conveyed whether the root was to be understood as a noun, verb, adjective, or adverb; they specified cases, voices, moods, and tenses, and so on. Thus, a relatively small number of agreed roots could quickly be transformed into a character in which an entire language could be written: 'whereby two, although not understanding one the others language, yet by the helpe thereof, may communicate their minds one to another' (title-page). As a sample of his common writing, Lodwick provided a transcript of the opening eight verses of the first chapter of St John's Gospel (illustrated opposite). The symbols of the common writing were reminiscent of musical notation, and Lodwick eventually intended them to be accompanied by numbers which would identify their roots in a lexicon which he promised to compose.

Lodwick's *Common Writing* was published by Hartlib, and attracted favourable notice from Boyle and from Sir Cheney Culpeper. They appear, however, to

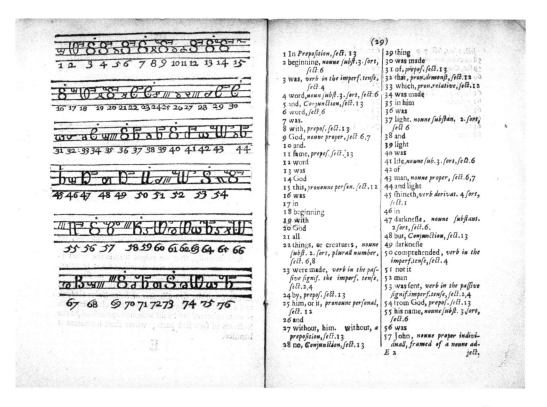

Figure 39
Eight verses from the first chapter of St John's Gospel, written in Francis Lodwick's 'common writing', displayed next to the numerical key which he composed for it. Lodwick was the first person to outline a design for a universal character.
Catalogue no. 41, pp. 28–29.

have been more intrigued by the concept of a universal character than they were convinced by Lodwick's execution of it. There were numerous drawbacks with schemes such as Lodwick's, for example: how were things to be analysed so that an agreed lexicon of accurately-chosen roots might be made; how was such a lexicon to be disseminated so that the ideal of universal communication could be achieved? Nevertheless, Lodwick's work was valued by others who attempted to compose universal languages, especially Wilkins, who asked Lodwick to help him with the orthography of his real character (see catalogue no. 43).

Vivian Salmon, *The Works of Francis Lodwick* (London, 1972); M. M. Slaughter, *Universal Languages and Scientific Taxonomy in the Seventeenth Century* (Cambridge, 1982), pp. 116–20; Thomas Birch (ed.), *The Works of the Honourable Robert Boyle* (new edition, 6 vols, London, 1772), vol. 1, pp. xxxvii–viii; M. J. Braddick and Mark Greengrass (eds.), 'The Letters of Sir Cheney Culpeper, 1641–1657', pp. 105–402 in *Camden Miscellany XXXIII* (Camden Society, Fifth Series, vol. 7, 1996), pp. 288–9 & 292–4.

The Tower

42. George Dalgarno
Ars signorum, vulgo character universalis et lingua philosophice
London, 1661
8°: A–I⁸
117 × 72 mm
Savile Cc 18

George Dalgarno (1626?–87), who was born in Aberdeen and educated at Marischal College, appears to have a kept a private grammar school in Oxford from the mid-1650s. He also worked as a shorthand tutor, and soon came into contact with John Wilkins and Seth Ward (1617–89), the Savilian professor of astronomy.

Dalgarno originally sought to develop an improved, international shorthand, building on earlier models and based on a core vocabulary of significant symbols. His work was encouraged by Wilkins, who was developing his own ideas about a universal language at the same time, and he was taken up by Hartlib, who hoped that Dalgarno's shorthand might form the basis for a real character. In his excitement, Hartlib responded enthusiastically to a specimen giving John 16: 1–13 in Dalgarno's character: 'it is so exact and compendious that the whole Bible will be printed in 9 or 10 sheets' (British Library, Ms. Add. 4377, fol. 149r).

Dalgarno spent part of 1657 living at Hartlib's house in London, and published proposals for a universal character that 'shall immediately represent things, and not the sounds of Words' (British Library, Ms. Add. 4377, fol. 143r). Hartlib publicized Dalgarno's work extensively at home and abroad, and several of his correspondents gave their opinions of it. Lodwick approved a scheme which was similar to some of his own designs, although he criticized Dalgarno's method for writing the character. Both John Beale and Robert Wood were sure that Dalgarno's efforts would lead to an improved shorthand, but were, in Wood's words, 'not convinced that it will answer those ends proposed, at least not under a great many yeares' (Letter to Hartlib, 8th August ? 1657, *Hartlib Papers*, 33/1/25A–26B). Sir Cheney Culpeper (1611–63), who offered to patronize Dalgarno, asked 'Yf Mr Dalgarnoes Characters be non ad placitum imponentis [not placed according to whim], but rationally significante vsque at summos apices [down to the last jot], my next question woulde be whether it be not the same with Adams langwage & (yf not) whether there might not be (a radice) a thirde character framed more easy to the hande & yet as comprehensiue' (Letter to Hartlib, 20th September 1657, transcribed in Braddick and Greengrass, p. 375). Such uncertainty characterized other responses to Dalgarno's work, and, although plenty of interest was expressed in his schemes, he did not receive the patronage which Hartlib sought for him.

By 1661, Dalgarno had redesigned his plans for a universal language along lines that were similar to those which Wilkins was also following. Jealous of his priority, and still eager for support, Dalgarno published his new scheme in *Ars signorum*. This was a proper real character, rather than a form of abbreviated writing, which was based not on an agreed lexicon but on a taxonomy of things. Although Dalgarno's classificatory system was old-fashioned and had only been worked out at an initial level, this was nevertheless a new departure. The opening dedication to Charles II in this copy has been translated into English (see figure 36). It expresses the hope that the King will support 'invention & improvement of Arts which make a Nation famous honoured & admired'.

Dalgarno was quite explicit about the religious motivation for seeking a universal language, which would assist in the propagation of the Gospel and bring about 'the releife of the confusion of languages' (British Library, Ms. Add. 4377, fol. 144r). A philosophical language would also improve the communications of the soul, which has to express itself via language.

Dalgarno's original plans to reform shorthand had been inspired partly by his knowledge of the grammar of Hebrew. Although he abandoned that project, the Bible and its language continued to provide Dalgarno with historical precedents for the success of a real character. *Ars signorum* included a rendering of the first chapter of Genesis in Dalgarno's language (pp. 118–21), and elsewhere Dalgarno remarked on the perfection of the historical account of language to be found in Genesis. Events described in Genesis also underwrote Dalgarno's taxonomy (Christ Church, Ms. 162, fol. 82):

> God himself named Adam thoe a single individuu[m] and the most perfect of all corporal beings by a derivative not a primitive word. Adam as a perfect Philosopher following nature and the example of his maker gave names to all living creatures not primitive and independent words being antendently to this imposition meer insignificant sounds, but words of a secondary constitution inflected from other words, ye primary and proper sense of which contributed to the describing of the nature of [tha]t thing whereof it was to be the name or which it was to represent.

Dalgarno argued that the Fall had corrupted the original language of Adam, but that the pure Hebrew which had been spoken by Noah and his descendants had initially preserved much of that real character. However, the confusion of languages which took place at the Tower of Babel was, for Dalgarno, a dreadful miracle, in which new mother tongues were created by God to disperse mankind, and after which Hebrew, like all other languages, was subject to continual decay.

These were the curses which the real character, by purifying understandings as well as increasing communication, might help to lift.

Vivian Salmon, *The Study of Language in 17th-Century England* (2nd edition, Amsterdam, 1988), pp. 157–75; David Cram, 'Universal Language Schemes in Seventeenth-Century Britain', *Histoire Epistémologie Langage*, vol. 7 (1985), pp. 35–44; M. M. Slaughter, *Universal Languages and Scientific Taxonomy in the Seventeenth Century* (Cambridge, 1982), pp. 121-3 & 141-53; M. J. Braddick and Mark Greengrass (eds.), 'The Letters of Sir Cheney Culpeper, 1641-1657', pp. 105-402 in *Camden Miscellany XXXIII* (Camden Society, Fifth Series, vol. 7, 1996), pp. 374-7; British Library, Ms. Add. 4377 (Papers of John Pell); Christ Church Oxford, Ms. 162 (Notebook and autobiography of George Dalgarno); *Hartlib Papers*, 7/128/1A-B, 33/1/25A-26B, 39/3/27A, 42/7/1A-2B, 49/1/1A-3B, 52/14A-15B, 56/1/74A-75B, 56/2/1A-2B.

43. John Wilkins
An Essay Towards a Real Character and a Philosophical Language
London, 1668
fol. in 4s: π^2 a–d^2 B–3M^4 3a^4 3A–3T^4
252 × 127mm
L 2.14 Art.

According to John Wallis (1616-1703), cryptographer and Savilian Professor of Geometry, Dalgarno's *Ars signorum* gave John Wilkins the idea for his work on the real character. However, despite Dalgarno's suggestions of plagiarism, it seems more likely that Wilkins began working on his ideas in collaboration with Seth Ward during the mid-1650s, co-opting Dalgarno later in the decade.

Wilkins differed with Dalgarno over the method for constructing the taxonomies which underlay the real character. In particular, Wilkins realized that the number of taxonomical categories would have to be greater than was proposed by Dalgarno, and that the taxonomy would have to be constructed in a hierarchical order so that its categories would eventually relate to, and name, all things. As Dalgarno himself recognized, Wilkins was able to undertake this more ambitious project because he could call on a wide range of assistance from his friends and clients. In particular, Wilkins was able to obtain information from several other Fellows of the Royal Society during the early 1660s, which allowed him to expand his coverage of the natural world and the mechanical arts. Thus, John Ray (1627-1705) assisted Wilkins in drawing up new tables of plants and animals; Samuel Pepys communicated information on naval affairs; and Francis Lodwick helped with orthography. The alphabetical dictionary which completed Wilkins' work, and which could be used to locate English words within its

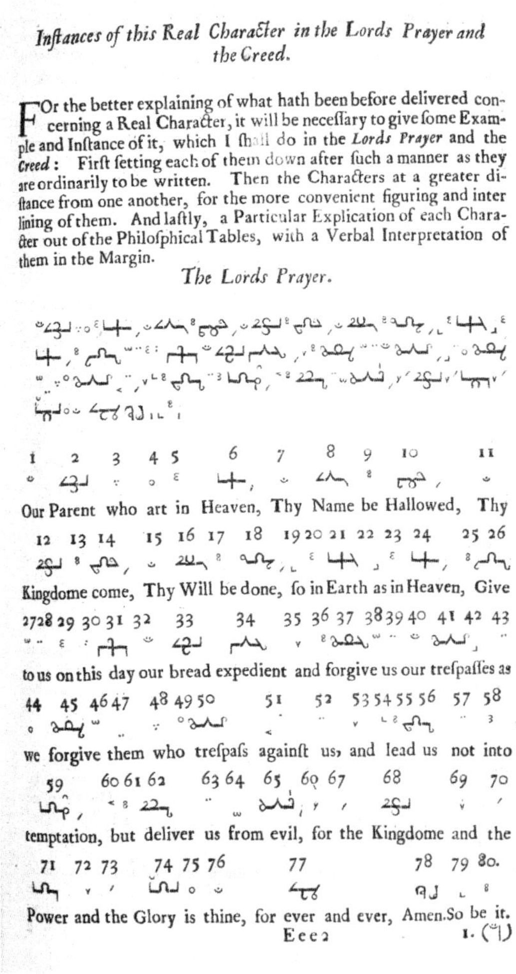

Inſtances of this Real Character in the Lords Prayer and the Creed.

FOr the better explaining of what hath been before delivered concerning a Real Character, it will be neceſſary to give ſome Example and Inſtance of it, which I ſhall do in the *Lords Prayer* and the *Creed*: Firſt ſetting each of them down after ſuch a manner as they are ordinarily to be written. Then the Characters at a greater diſtance from one another, for the more convenient figuring and interlining of them. And laſtly, a Particular Explication of each Character out of the Philoſphical Tables, with a Verbal Interpretation of them in the Margin.

The Lords Prayer.

1 2 3 4 5 6 7 8 9 10 11
Our Parent who art in Heaven, Thy Name be Hallowed, Thy

12 13 14 15 16 17 18 19 20 21 22 23 24 25 26
Kingdome come, Thy Will be done, ſo in Earth as in Heaven, Give

27 28 29 30 31 32 33 34 35 36 37 38 39 40 41 42 43
to us on this day our bread expedient and forgive us our treſpaſſes as

44 45 46 47 48 49 50 51 52 53 54 55 56 57 58
we forgive them who treſpaſs againſt us, and lead us not into

59 60 61 62 63 64 65 66 67 68 69 70
temptation, but deliver us from evil, for the Kingdome and the

71 72 73 74 75 76 77 78 79 80.
Power and the Glory is thine, for ever and ever, Amen.So be it.

Eee 2 I. (^1)

Figure 40

The Lord's Prayer in John Wilkins' real character. Wilkins was concerned to make his character elegant and concise as well as to ensure that it was suitable for universal application. The choice of the Lord's Prayer as an example of the use of the character is not insignificant, given the biblical inspiration behind the creation of universal languages and their potential use by missionaries. Catalogue no. 43, p. 395.

philosophical tables, was compiled by William Lloyd (1627–1717), who had been a private tutor at Wadham in the late 1650s. The resulting work was a complex analysis of language and an attempt at a real character based on an wide-ranging empirical classification of the natural world. After Wilkins' death in 1672, efforts continued to be made to revise and extend his work, although, in time, the limitations of its approach, which assumed a direct and logical relationship between words and things, became clear.

Wilkins regarded the confusion of tongues at Babel as representing the historical point of origin of modern human languages. He was, however, sceptical of the efforts of his contemporaries to classify the resulting families of languages. He also realized that languages themselves changed over time, and felt that the

The Tower

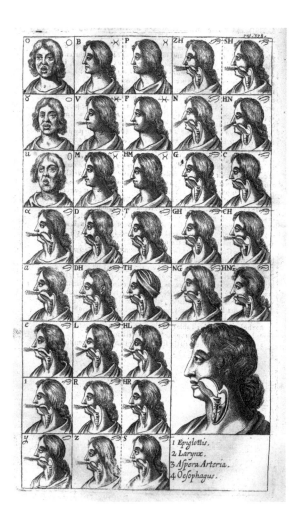

Figure 41
Table illustrating the production of speech in the throat and the mouth, from John Wilkins' *Essay Towards a Real Character and a Philosophical Language*. Like Dalgarno and John Wallis, Wilkins was concerned with analysing speech and finding a method to teach the deaf and the dumb to talk. He believed that his real character and philosophical language might be a means towards that end.
Catalogue no. 43, p. 379.

original language of Adam in paradise had been completely lost (pp. 2–5). This provided one of the stimuli for inventing an artificial real character, in which empirical knowledge could be used to reconstruct a version of the order of nature that had been revealed to Adam. Wilkins was concerned to produce a character which was attractive and concise, as well as having the potential for universal application. These were all factors which might recommend the real character as a tool for missionary activity. For this and other reasons, it is unsurprising that Wilkins chose the Lord's Prayer (see figure 40, p. 116) and the Creed as sample texts for translation into his character.

M. M. Slaughter, *Universal Languages and Scientific Taxonomy in the Seventeenth Century* (Cambridge, 1982), pp. 157–86; Christ Church Oxford, Ms. 162 (Notebook and autobiography of George Dalgarno), fols. 20–42.

The Tower

Figure 42
The frontispiece of Cave Beck's *Universal Character*, showing the figures of Europe, Asia, Africa and America. They greet each other with 'dumb Signes' and, predictably enough, elect Europe as their 'Speaker'. Catalogue no. 44.

44. Cave Beck
The Universal Character
London, 1657
8°: A-M⁸
140 × 84 mm
Broxb. 100.28

Among those who sent their ideas for a universal character to John Wilkins during the 1650s was the Ipswich schoolmaster, Cave Beck (1623–1706). Beck's work, which was disparaged by Dalgarno as 'nothing else, but an enigmatical way of writing the English language' (Letter to Hartlib, 20th April 1657, British Library, Ms. Add. 4377, fol. 148r), aimed to facilitate communication by providing a largely numerical character which could be read off in any language. It contained little grammatical analysis, and was never equipped with the philosophical dictionary which Beck envisaged (along the lines of Comenius's *Janua linguarum*, see catalogue no. 39). Instead, the characters were keyed to a simple list of 3,996 primitive English words. The meaning of these roots could

The Tower

be modified to produce a variety of derived nouns and their cases by the addition of coded letters to the basic number of the root. Beck also suggested a primitive system by which the letters and numbers could be vocalized. Beck hoped that his work would promote trade, and make the work of converting native peoples to Christianity easier. He saw its principal advantage as being its simplicity, and the supposed ease with which it could be learned.

Many of the laudatory poems prefixed to Beck's work mention the curse of Babel, and hope, rather optimistically, that the universal character might overcome the confusion of tongues. The verses, by 'E. K.', which accompany the frontispiece urge the peoples of the world to unite under Europe's direction and agree to build Sion, in place of Babel. The frontispiece itself shows figures representing Africa, America, Asia and Europe grouped around a table. According to E. K.'s verses, they greet each other with 'dumb Signes', and elect Europe as 'Speaker'. Europe holds a piece of paper on which are written the numbers '2356'. These translate as 'to hunt' in Beck's character, which might be a (somewhat ominous) reference to Nimrod, the builder of Babel and 'a mighty hunter before the Lord' (Genesis 10: 9), but is perhaps more likely to be an engraver's error!

Vivian Salmon, *The Study of Language in 17th-Century England* (2nd edition, Amsterdam, 1988), pp. 176-90; Vivian Salmon, *The Works of Francis Lodwick* (London, 1972), pp. 18-19 & 131; M. M. Slaughter, *Universal Languages and Scientific Taxonomy in the Seventeenth Century* (Cambridge, 1982), pp. 120-1; British Library, Ms. Add. 4377 (Papers of John Pell).

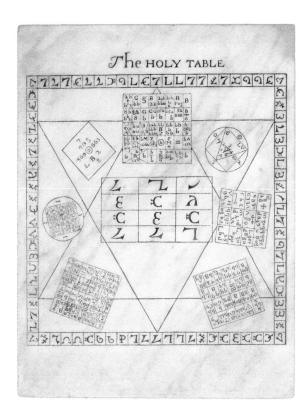

Figure 43
Marble copy of John Dee's 'holy table', the original constructed by him in wood according to the direction of 'angelic spirits' delivered through the medium Edward Kelly. Catalogue no. 45.

45. John Dee's Holy Table
    Unsigned, late 17th century
    600 × 463 mm
    Museum of the History of Science, Inv. no. 15,449

This is a marble copy of the 'holy table' constructed by John Dee in 1582 following the instructions of the angel Uriel, whose attendance had been effected with the assistance of Dee's 'skryer' Edward Kelly. The characters inside the diagram belong to Dee's 'Enochian Alphabet'.

The diagram of the holy table was published by Meric Casaubon in 1659. This marble version was presented to the Bodleian Library in 1750 by Richard Rawlinson, according to whom it had previously belonged to the astrologer William Lilly.

The Tower

46. Athanasius Kircher
Turris Babel
Amsterdam, 1679
fol. in 4s: *-2*⁴ A-2F⁴ (with 28 plates, some folding)
275 × 155 mm
Vet. B3 b. 33

In succession to his reconstruction of the history of the Ark (catalogue no. 37), the Jesuit Athanasius Kircher (1601–80) attempted a similar history of the Tower of Babel. This traced events following the Deluge, as the sons of Noah moved eastwards from Ararat to the plain of Shinar (Genesis 11: 2). It described the building of the Tower of Babel, under the tyranny of Nimrod, which had required the work of fifty thousand men, and argued that, despite such effort, it was impossible for this very high building to have reached to the moon, as some had suggested. Using evidence derived from Annius of Viterbo's spurious amplification of the history of Berossos, Kircher also proposed that Nimrod's successors as rulers of Babylon had erected a temple in the form of a tower on the ruins of his structure. Following the Jewish historian Josephus, Kircher argued that the original builders of the Tower were seeking protection from future inundations, having recently descended from the safety of the mountains of Ararat to the flat lands of Shinar, and that, as descendants of Ham (the son whose offspring Noah had cursed) they were afraid of attack or of divine punishment. He suggested that God had frustrated this attempt to escape from his power by confusing the speech of the builders of Babel.

Kircher's main interest in *Turris Babel* was with the history of language. He rejected the view that God had made every one of the builders of Babel speak a different language. Instead, the original language, Hebrew, was preserved only in the pure line of Shem and his descendants, and four new tongues began to be spoken by the descendants of the other sons of Noah. The placing of linguistic barriers between families led to the dispersion of peoples, and the settlement of the whole world. In time, the five basic language families themselves split or decayed, leading, Kircher argued, to the existence of seventy-two mother tongues, to which all contemporary languages related. For much of *Turris Babel*, Kircher concentrates on the history of the Semitic tongues and of writing in the Near East. His discussion of these topics is used as the basis for a Christianized comparative mythology. Here, Kircher built on his earlier work on hieroglyphics, which argued that they were the secret writing of Egyptian priests, and encoded knowledge of the one, true God.

Arno Borst, *Der Turmbau von Babel*, (4 vols. in 6 parts, Stuttgart, 1957–63, reprinted Munich, 1995), vol. 3, part 1, pp. 1368–70; Don Cameron Allen, *Mysteriously Meant* (Baltimore, 1970), pp. 119–33.

The Tower

47. Sir Thomas Browne
*Pseudodoxia epidemica: or, Enquiries into Very
Many Received Tenents, and Commonly Preserved Truths*
London, 1646
fol. in 4s: a⁶ b⁴ A–3A⁴ 3B⁶
222 × 140 mm
O 2.26 Art. Seld.

Sir Thomas Browne (1605–82) followed up the publishing success of his *Religio medici* of 1642 with a work devoted to disproving a number of 'vulgar errors' and commonly believed misconceptions. *Pseudodoxia epidemica* discussed erroneous beliefs about the natural world (minerals, vegetables, animals, and the human body) and those which arose from human society and culture (pictures, geography, and history, including scriptural history).

One of the errors treated by Browne was the belief that 'the Tower of *Babel* was erected against a second Deluge' (pp. 348–9). Browne set out the evidence for this opinion, which was drawn principally from Josephus (and which was accepted by Kircher, see catalogue no. 46). Although he was willing to credit Berossos' accounts of the towers of Babylon, Browne denied that the Tower of Babel could ever have been built tall enough to provide a defence against supernatural flooding. He also suggested that it was implausible that people who were afraid of a second deluge should ever have descended from the safety of the mountains to live in an area as prone to natural inundation as Mesopotamia. In any case, Browne pointed out, a correct, historical reading of scripture precluded the interpretation that the Tower was built to avoid a second Flood. God had promised Noah (Genesis 9: 11–17) that he would never destroy the world again in that way, and had made the rainbow a sign of his renewed covenant with mankind, of which that promise was a part. Browne thought it unlikely that, within a few generations, Noah's descendants would have forgotten this promise. Instead, he argued that the building of the Tower had been part of Nimrod's secret plan to establish his own dominon over people, and a symbol of the tyranny with which he ruled his subjects. Nimrod had promised the builders of the Tower that they would be famous, in order to dupe them into constructing a terrible city from which he could rule. Through the confusion of tongues, God had frustrated Nimrod's plot to dominate mankind.

Not all of Browne's readers were convinced by this argument. This copy of *Pseudodoxia epidemica* belonged to Dr Christopher Wren (1591–1658), Dean of Windsor and father of the scientific prodigy and future architect, Christopher Wren (see catalogue nos. 60 and 65). The elder Wren annotated this book extensively, mentioning ideas for a universal language at one point, and picking up

Figure 44
Among the most impressive features of Athanasius Kircher's *Turris Babel* were its illustrations, engraved by C. Decker, a German craftsman resident in Amsterdam. The plate of the Tower of Babel itself was based on a drawing by Lievin Cruyl (*c.* 1640–1720), a Flemish artist who worked largely in Rome. The spiral design of the Tower is reminiscent of the archaeological remains of Mesopotamian temple towers, and is taller and thinner than the designs of Matthaeus Merian or of Pieter Bruegel and his imitators.
Catalogue no. 46, plate between pp. 40 and 41.

The Tower

47. Sir Thomas Browne
*Pseudodoxia epidemica: or, Enquiries into Very
Many Received Tenents, and Commonly Preserved Truths*
London, 1646
fol. in 4s: a⁶ b⁴ A–3A⁴ 3B⁶
222 × 140 mm
O 2.26 Art. Seld.

Sir Thomas Browne (1605–82) followed up the publishing success of his *Religio medici* of 1642 with a work devoted to disproving a number of 'vulgar errors' and commonly believed misconceptions. *Pseudodoxia epidemica* discussed erroneous beliefs about the natural world (minerals, vegetables, animals, and the human body) and those which arose from human society and culture (pictures, geography, and history, including scriptural history).

One of the errors treated by Browne was the belief that 'the Tower of *Babel* was erected against a second Deluge' (pp. 348–9). Browne set out the evidence for this opinion, which was drawn principally from Josephus (and which was accepted by Kircher, see catalogue no. 46). Although he was willing to credit Berossos' accounts of the towers of Babylon, Browne denied that the Tower of Babel could ever have been built tall enough to provide a defence against supernatural flooding. He also suggested that it was implausible that people who were afraid of a second deluge should ever have descended from the safety of the mountains to live in an area as prone to natural inundation as Mesopotamia. In any case, Browne pointed out, a correct, historical reading of scripture precluded the interpretation that the Tower was built to avoid a second Flood. God had promised Noah (Genesis 9: 11–17) that he would never destroy the world again in that way, and had made the rainbow a sign of his renewed covenant with mankind, of which that promise was a part. Browne thought it unlikely that, within a few generations, Noah's descendants would have forgotten this promise. Instead, he argued that the building of the Tower had been part of Nimrod's secret plan to establish his own dominon over people, and a symbol of the tyranny with which he ruled his subjects. Nimrod had promised the builders of the Tower that they would be famous, in order to dupe them into constructing a terrible city from which he could rule. Through the confusion of tongues, God had frustrated Nimrod's plot to dominate mankind.

Not all of Browne's readers were convinced by this argument. This copy of *Pseudodoxia epidemica* belonged to Dr Christopher Wren (1591–1658), Dean of Windsor and father of the scientific prodigy and future architect, Christopher Wren (see catalogue nos. 60 and 65). The elder Wren annotated this book extensively, mentioning ideas for a universal language at one point, and picking up on Browne's discussion of events at Babel. In his note, Wren points out that Nimrod and his people were descended from Ham, the son whom Noah had cursed. He argued that they were likely to have forgotten God's promise never to repeat the Flood, which was only preserved in the families of Shem and Japhet, Noah's other sons. This was especially likely since Ham's descendants had 'now forgot God himself as appears by this bold attemp[t]'.

To Wren, the building of the Tower of Babel was a sign of human pride and folly, which had been ordered by Nimrod, who had also abandoned true religion for idolatry. This was a different reading of the Bible from that which Browne advanced, and it was perhaps prompted by a greater deference to other ancient sources (such as Josephus) than was shown by Browne. Yet, although they gave different weight to the various parts of the narrative of the Tower of Babel, both Browne's and Wren's interpretations derived from a literal reading of the biblical story and an attempt to interpret it as history.

Geoffrey Keynes, *A Bibliography of Sir Thomas Browne* (2nd edition, Oxford, 1968), p. 55; Rosalie L. Colie, 'Dean Wren's Marginalia and Early Science at Oxford', *Bodleian Library Record*, vol. 5 (1954–6), pp. 541–51.

48. Richard Verstegan
    A Restitution of Decayed Intelligence in Antiquities
    3rd edition, London, 1634
    4°: *–3*⁴ A–2X⁴
    152 × 90 mm
    B 19. 10 Linc.

Unlike Sir Thomas Browne, many seventeenth-century readers of Genesis 11 were happy to take Josephus as their guide. In the opening chapter of *A Restitution of Decayed Intelligence in Antiquities*, Richard Verstegan (originally Rowlands) (*fl.* 1565–1620) used Josephus's work to argue that all three sons of Noah and their descendants were reluctant to leave the mountains around Ararat, and had to be admonished by God to do so and to people the world. This divine reproof led them to fear a second Flood, and consequently to accept Nimrod's leadership when he offered them the chance of protection through the building of the Tower of Babel.

However, Verstegan was less interested in the events which had taken place at Babel, than in the dispersion of peoples which followed from them. He argued

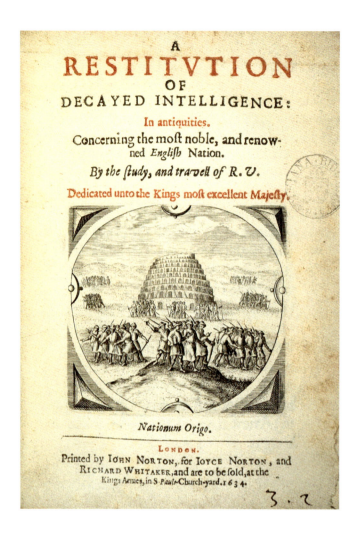

Figure 45
The title-page of Richard Verstegan's *Restitution of Decayed Intelligence*. The work was concerned with the dispersion of peoples after the confusion of tongues at Babel, in particular the Saxon ancestry of the English people. Illustrated with engravings by the author himself, it was frequently reprinted and helped to establish the Tower of Babel as a point of origin for modern nationhood.
From catalogue no. 48.

that seventy-two national or linguistic groups had been created by the confusion of tongues, and that they spread themselves across Asia, Africa, and Europe. Verstegan's main concern lay with the line of Japhet, whose descendants moved into Europe, and, in particular, with Japhet's son Gomer and his son and grandson, Ashkenaz and Tuisco, from whom, he argued, the Germanic nations were descended. For this part of his argument, Verstegan was heavily dependent on Annius of Viterbo's spurious amplification of the history of Berossos. The bulk of *A Restitution of Decayed Intelligence in Antiquities*, however, was devoted to the Saxon ancestry of the English people, and its influence on the language and customs of Britain.

A Restitution of Decayed Intelligence in Antiquities was first published in Antwerp in 1605. Although Verstegan's choice of sources was not always particularly original, his work was remarkable for rejecting the idea of a Trojan, or even British, origin for English customs, and for asserting the Germanic heritage of the English people. During the course of the seventeenth century, there were many other writers who, whilst differing from his conclusions, followed Verstegan in seeking the origins of the people of Britain in the line of Gomer. Verstegan's work, strikingly illustrated with cuts engraved by the author himself, was reprinted frequently. It helped to establish the image of the Tower of Babel as the point of origin for modern nationhood, even for the inhabitants of far-flung islands off Europe's western shore.

A. F. Allison and D. M. Rogers, *The Contemporary Printed Literature of the English Counter-Reformation between 1558 and 1640* (2 vols, Aldershot, 1989–94), vol. 2, p. 151; Graham Parry, *The Trophies of Time* (Oxford, 1995), pp. 49–69; Stuart Piggott, *Ruins in a Landscape* (Edinburgh, 1976), pp. 55–76.

49. Thomas Thorowgood
Iewes in America, or, Probabilities that the Americans Are of that Race
London, 1650
4°: π^1 a–e^4 B–S^4 T^1
152 × 95 mm
Wood 637 (1)

Thomas Thorowgood (1595–1669) was a Norfolk minister who was sent as a delegate to the Westminster Assembly of Divines, which met from 1643 to 1649. Active in London during the mid-1640s, he was an associate of Hartlib's collaborator, John Dury (see catalogue nos. 66 and 67). Thorowgood was sympathetic to Presbyterian attempts to reform the Church of England, and, unlike Dury, refused to swear the Engagement oath (thought by many Presbyterians to breach the terms of earlier undertakings which they had given). Thorowgood depended for some years on the patronage of the Fairfax family, and, although he later acted in support of the regime during the mid-1650s, he claimed after 1660 to have been disillusioned with political affairs ever since the execution of Charles I in 1649. Some evidence for this assertion can be found in the publishing history of *Iewes in America*. The second edition of the work (published in 1660) contains a dedication to Charles II, which, according to testimony signed by Dury among others, was originally intended for Charles I. This dedication was suppressed in November 1648, and, when Thorowgood's work was first published in 1650, it was addressed to the gentry of Norfolk.

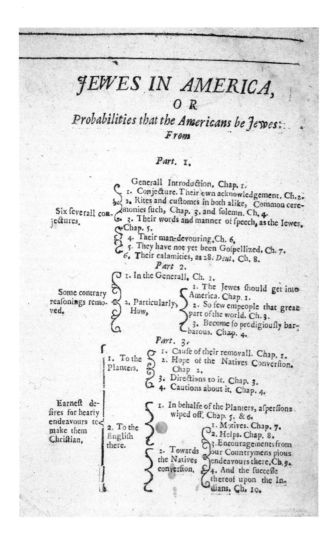

Figure 46

Outline contents of Thomas Thorowgood's *Iewes in America*. Thorowgood argued that the native Americans were close relatives of the Jews, descended from Noah through Shem and his offspring who had journeyed eastward from Ararat soon after the landing of the Ark. Catalogue no. 49, facing title-page.

Thorowgood was inspired by reports of the work of John Eliot (1604–90), minister of Roxbury, Massachusetts, who had begun to preach to the local Natick Indians in their own language in 1646. With the aid of the Corporation for Promoting and Propagating the Gospel among the Indians in New England (established with Parliamentary support in 1649), Eliot sought to establish 'praying towns' of Indian converts and potential converts. Eliot's own letters, published in the second edition of *Iewes in America*, revealed the biblical and millenarian foundations of his work. He argued that Shem and his sons had journeyed eastwards from Ararat in the years following the landing of the Ark, whilst Ham and Japhet and their descendants had remained with Noah. Eventually, Nimrod had rebelled and set out with some followers in search of the site of Eden. Nimrod's ambitions, culminating in the building of the Tower of Babel, had led to the dispersion of peoples, which had primarily affected the descendants of Ham and Japhet. Shem and his offspring had already obeyed God's command to people the earth, and had occupied the eastern part of the world, including India, China, and the Americas.

According to Eliot, then, the native Americans were close relatives of the Jews, and their conversion would help to bring the whole world into the Christian fold and hasten the last days. This was an interpretation which Thorowgood echoed in *Iewes in America*, where (following Verstegan and others) he argued that language and custom held the key to the origins of nations. He suggested that the speech, legends, and customs of the native peoples of both North and South America indicated that they shared common ancestry with the Jews. He urged people to support Eliot's work on the grounds that the Gospel had to spread to all nations, and the Jews convert to Christianity, before Christ would come again to judge and rule over his people.

Iewes in America contained a preface consisting of a letter by John Dury, dated 27th January, 1650. Here, Dury mentioned a number of travellers' tales then circulating in Amsterdam, which told of the discovery of lost tribes of Jews. The most striking of these had been explained to Dury by Menasseh ben Israel (see catalogue no. 50) and described a tribe of lost Jews living in South America. Thorowgood included a translation of the full account of this episode, sent by Menasseh to Dury, at the end of *Iewes in America*. Dury's preface took up the theme of the possible future conversion of the Jews, mentioning also the Jewish belief that the Messiah might come once the Jews were scattered to all the corners of the earth. According to both Dury and Thorowgood, the time was coming when the dispersion of peoples and the confusion of tongues would be reversed, and all God's people would be called together to live under a single law.

Thomas Thorowgood, *Jews in America* (2nd edition, London, 1660); B. Cozens-Hardy, 'A Puritan Moderate: Dr. Thomas Thorowgood, S. T. B., 1595 to 1669, Rector of Grimston, Little Massingham and Great Cressingham', *Norfolk Archaeology*, vol. 22 (1923-5), pp. 311-37; Jean M. O'Brien, *Dispossession by Degrees: Indian Land and Identity in Natick, Massachusetts, 1650-1790* (Cambridge, 1997), pp. 26-64.

50. Menasseh ben Israel
מקוה ישראל *Hoc est, spes Israelis*
Amsterdam, 1650
8°: π⁶ A–G⁸
124 × 65 mm
8° M 32 Th. Seld.

As a leading figure in the nation of the Portuguese Jews in Amsterdam, and one of the rabbis of the community, Menasseh ben Israel (1604–57) came to the attention of Samuel Hartlib and his friends during the 1640s. In particular, Menasseh's approval was sought for the work of Dury's friend, Adam Boreel, on a vocalized edition of the Mishnah. At the same time, Dury, who was resident in Rotterdam, began collecting travellers' tales about the dispersal of the tribes of Israel into the east and west. Initially, Dury was most interested in the possibility that more accurate copies of the Hebrew scriptures might have been preserved among such people (for this reason, he was also concerned to find out about the Caraites). However, as accounts of the lost tribes multiplied, both Dury and his Jewish informants began to see them in a messianic light.

Menasseh himself had composed several messianic treatises during the 1640s, and it was he who interviewed the refugee, Antonio de Montezinos, in 1644 and 1645, gathering from him an account of a tribe of Jewish Indians, descendants of Reuben, who lived in the depths of New Granada (modern Colombia), in South America. Menasseh soon communicated his discovery to Dury, and both men interpreted Montezinos' information in the light of their hopes for the coming of the Messiah. For Menasseh, the Israelites in America were a separate people, whose existence indicated that there were Jews to be found on every continent, suggesting that the diaspora was complete, and that the messianic age was about to dawn. Dury saw the Jewish Indians in a different light, as potential converts whose inclusion into the Christian fold might fulfil the prophecies of the book of Daniel, and usher in the rule of Christ's saints.

Montezinos' tales form part of the account of the extent of the Jewish diaspora given in Menasseh's *Hope of Israel*, which was published in 1650. Two editions of the book were produced, with differing contents. One, in Spanish, was aimed at Jewish readers, and included material on the messianic redemption of the Jews not printed elsewhere. The other, in Latin, was distributed more widely, and quickly translated into English by Moses Wall. Encouraged by Dury, Menasseh dedicated his work to the Parliament of England. Both Menasseh and Dury were interested in the possibility of bringing about the return of the Jews to England, an event which finally took place in 1656. Menasseh hoped to widen the trading contacts of the Amsterdam Jews, and also to broaden the Diaspora in order to hasten the fulfilment of prophecy. Dury, who was at times rather tentative about the scheme, wanted the Jews admitted to England so that they could be subjected to an organized programme of proselytizing, and brought to the Christian faith.

Menasseh ben Israel, *The Hope of Israel*, edited Henry Méchoulan and Gérard Nahon, translated by Richenda George (Oxford, 1987); Yosef Kaplan, Henry Méchoulan, and Richard H. Popkin (eds.), *Menasseh ben Israel and his World* (Leiden, 1989); David S. Katz, *Philo-Semitism and the Readmission of the Jews to England 1603–1655* (Oxford, 1982), pp. 127-57; University Library, Amsterdam, Ms. III E. 9, number 76; *Hartlib Papers*, 3/2/127A-128B, 3/3/32A-33B.

Figure 47
Montano's design for the Temple, from his *Antiquitatum Iudaicarum* of 1593.
Unlike many designs of the period, Montano's proposal is thoroughly
realizable and interpreted in an architectural style familiar to him.
From catalogue no. 28.

THE TEMPLE

Any quest for the historical Temple of Jerusalem begins with questions and choices. There were three material temples, and one visionary one. The original Temple built by Solomon is recorded in two separate descriptions, in Kings Book I and Chronicles Book II; it was destroyed by the Babylonians when Nebuchadnezzar carried the Israelites into exile. The second Temple was built by Zerubbabel in about 500 B.C., after the return from captivity, while the third was the work of Herod I in about 20 B.C. and was destroyed by the Romans in A.D. 70.

Ezekiel's vision of a temple came to him 'In the five and twentieth year of our captivity' (Ezekiel 40: 1) and is recorded in detail in nine chapters of his prophesy. In addition, the Tabernacle, the tent built as a divine sanctuary by Moses to accompany the Israelites on their journeys after leaving Egypt, raised many of the same issues as the Temple and established some of its later design features.

In the sixteenth and seventeenth centuries, the Temple was a prominent focus for expository concern. This interest was variously devotional, historical or millenarian: the rebuilding of the Temple was a condition of the Millennium, the thousand-year reign of Christ on earth. Other questions it raised were architectural, since here was a divine design for a place of worship, as well as mathematical. While the broader concerns explain the currency of Temple commentaries in the period, its relevance here

The Temple

stems more from the mathematical and architectural interest in the Temple, on its relationship to standards of measure, and on the figure of Solomon and his mastery of natural knowledge.

Like the Ark, the fascination with the design of the Temple in this context stemmed from its divine origin. God was the designer and architect. He had spoken to Moses alone on Mount Sinai and instructed him in the building of the Tabernacle. Solomon had received the design of the Temple from his father David, whom God had told to name Solomon as the builder of his house. Ezekiel was in exile in Babylon when 'the hand of the Lord was upon me, and brought me thither. In the visions of God brought he me into the land of Israel' (Ezekiel 40: 1–2).

The common thread that is immediately evident in each of these revelations is an emphasis on measurement. The various dimensions of the Tabernacle, the Ark of the Covenant and the altar are all given to Moses in cubits. Both accounts of Solomon's Temple give the dimensions of its structure and contents in great detail. The same is true of Ezekiel's vision, but here, since he is being shown a building rather than instructed in its construction, he is guided by a man 'with a line of flax in his hand, and a measuring reed' (Ezekiel 40: 3). This reed is 6 cubits long, but the cubit has an additional hand-breadth beyond the usual distance from elbow to finger-tip, and the way the guide, 'whose appearance was like the appearance of brass', demonstrates the Temple to Ezekiel is to take him round the site, like a surveyor with a pole, measuring all its features as they proceed.

These dimensions, reiterated with such deliberation in the scriptural accounts, must hold the key to a divine geometry. It was noted that they were in round figures and that sites of particular significance demonstrated special relationships: the most holy place in the Temple, for example, was a perfect cube. The design must evince the kind of harmony and relation that was the aim of all architecture. But only the dimensions were given, and those mostly in plan, so there was great scope for projecting an architecture on to these parameters.

A successful exercise would achieve not only an appreciation of the divine geometry, it would be a guide to sacred architecture today – either a blueprint for churches of the reformed faith seeking a Christian alternative to pagan forms, whether Greek or Gothic, or a justification of traditional styles. The Temple design was a prize, with a sectarian dimension to the contest. If it could be cited as the precedent for a sacred building, as it was, for example, for the monastery-palace of El Escorial built by Phillip II of Spain, spiritual as well as mathematical authority would accrue to the design. Phillip encouraged the Jesuit Villalpando (catalogue no. 51, illustrated overleaf) in his work of turning Ezekiel's vision of the Temple into a vast Renaissance palace reflecting the harmonic relationships of the cosmos. Villalpando's appropriation of the Temple was contested by other sectarian interests through the seventeenth century; indeed it was contested even before publication, by Montano (catalogue no. 28), who offered a more restrained and circumspect design.

The length of the cubit was essential to reconstructing the Temple, and there was more than one such unit of length. Other aspects of the scriptural account enforced this consideration of standards of measure. Ezekiel was told by his Temple guide (Ezekiel 45: 10-12):

> Ye shall have just balances, and a just ephah, and a just bath. The ephah and the bath shall be of one measure, that the bath may contain the tenth part of an homer, and the ephah the tenth part of an homer: the measure thereof shall be after the homer. And the shekel shall be twenty gerahs.

The ephah was a unit of dry measure, the bath was for liquid, while the shekel was a measure of weight as well as a coin. The detailed description of the contents of the Temple, for example the stated capacity in baths of a vessel whose dimensions are given in cubits, opened the way for the attempted recovery of the whole ancient Hebrew system of measures sanctioned by God.

The recovery of such measures had a spiritual dimension as well as a practical one. Just as languages had multiplied after Babel, so did measures. Now every city and province had individual standards, and even different ones for different goods. It was clear that God set great store by the proper regulation of measures and that the recovery of a universal standard would represent part of a progression towards the original Godly regulation of mankind or, in temporal terms, towards the New Jerusalem understood by many to be the object of Ezekiel's vision.

Like Adam before him and Noah, Solomon had a profound understanding of the natural world as a prominent part of the unparalleled wisdom for which he was celebrated. With knowledge came power and authority over nature, and not least the ability to raise so magnificent a building as the Temple. The image of Solomon as a natural historian was sanctioned by scripture (I Kings 4: 29-33):

> And God gave Solomon wisdom and understanding exceeding much, and largeness of heart, even as the sand that is on the sea shore. And Solomon's wisdom excelled the wisdom of all the children of the east country, and all the wisdom of Egypt. ... And he spake of trees, from the cedar tree that is in Lebanon even unto the hyssop that springeth out of the wall: he spake also of beasts, and of fowl, and of creeping things, and of fishes.

Solomon's command of natural knowledge and of nature herself was an influ-

The Temple

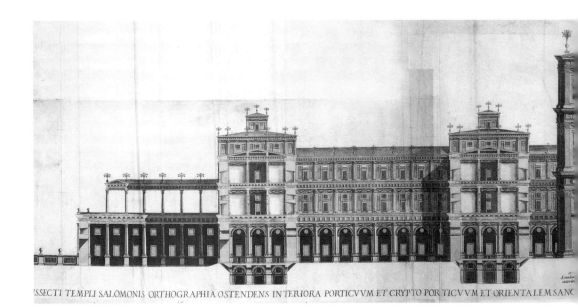
ISSECTI TEMPLI SALOMONIS ORTHOGRAPHIA OSTENDENS INTERIORA PORTICVVM ET CRYPTO PORTICVVM ET ORIENTALEM SANC

ential image. It was thought that he had written natural histories that had not survived, but the travellers whose story Bacon tells in his *New Atlantis* (catalogue no. 53) found that these precious books were treasured on the utopian island of Bensalem. Solomon's knowledge, unlike Adam's, was won through diligence and application. Adam had enjoyed an effortless knowledge of all things in his innocence in Eden, but natural histories had to be compiled through collection and organization. Bacon presented 'Salomon's House' as an institution for just such improvement through observation, experiment, organization and method. The call to such work was taken up by several groups and societies in seventeenth-century England, the best-known example being the Royal Society of London.

It is tempting to think that as the century progressed the mystical approach to the Temple declined. Samuel Lee, for example (catalogue no. 55), who was part of Wilkins' circle at Wadham College in the 1650s, had little time for the 'School of Pythagoras' tradition of Temple commentary. In France, Claude Perrault, in his famous treatise on the orders, sought to remove architectural rules from the authority of the sacred, and architectural history from the opinion of Villalpando 'qui pretend que Dieu par une inspiration particuliere a enseigné toutes ces proportions aux Architectes du Temple de Salomon' (Perrault, p. xviii). Christopher Wren also, on historical grounds, dismissed Villalpando's scheme as 'mere Fable' (catalogue no. 60).

The Temple

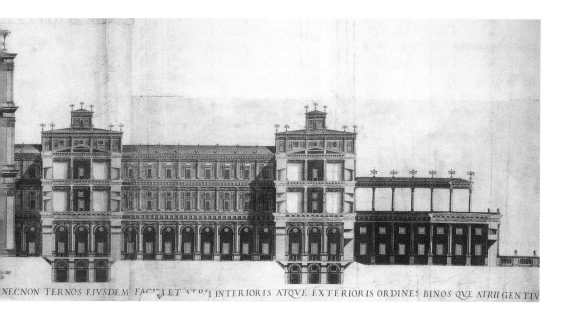

Figure 48
Villalpando's drawing, in section, of his extravagant design for the Temple, based on classical lines – an attempt in part to demonstrate the Judeo-Christian credentials of the pagan orders. Catalogue no. 51, plate facing p. 145.

For others, Ezekiel's description could still inspire a conjunction between practical mathematics, the language of angels, and a vision of the New Jerusalem. One such author was the independent minister Thomas Beverley, who in 1690, predicting the realization of Ezekiel's prophesy in 1697, wrote (Beverley, p. 9):

> And as Number, Weight, and Measure are so Essentially necessary to All the Great Things, that are perform'd in the World, as to Astronomy, Observation of the Heavens, and their Course, Geometry, Architecture, Statics, Navigation, Survey, Experimental Philosophy, and to all Commerce, and Traffick, and even mutual Cohabitation of Mankind; So under these Measures in this Vision are shaded the Sublimity of the Divine Communion with his Saints, and Servants; and of Angels, and Saints one with Another; and those Lines of Communication signified by Jacobs Ladder, Gen. 28.12. between the New Heaven, and the New Earth.

T. Beverley, *The Pattern of the Divine Temple* (London, 1690); C. Perrault, *Ordonnance des cinq especes de colonnes* (Paris, 1683).

The Temple

51. Hieronymo Prado and Juan Bautista Villalpando
    In Ezechiel explanationes et apparatus vrbis, ac templi Hierosolymitani
    3 vols, Rome, 1596–1605
    fol. in 6s: +–2+^{6} a–3H^6 (vol. 2)
    337 × 173 mm
    B 1.4 Th. Seld.

Perhaps the most famous and most controversial reconstruction of the Temple in the period was that due to the Spanish Jesuit Juan Bautista Villalpando. With fellow Jesuit Hieronymo Prado he began what would become a huge three-volume commentary on Ezekiel. However, after the first volume was published a dispute over the reconstruction of the Temple delayed further publication and, with the death of Prado, Villalpando worked on alone. Volume two, which appeared in 1605, contains his extraordinary illustrations of the Temple as a vast Renaissance palace in the classical idiom. The account was derived from Ezekiel's vision, but for Villalpando this was a guide also to Solomon's Temple, since both were designed by God.

With God as architect, the design of the Temple will reflect his other creations: the macrocosm of the world and the microcosm of man. Thus Villalpando incorporates aspects of the harmony and order of the heavens into the Temple, while its proportions also encode those of the human body. All these hidden relationships are derived from Ezekiel and expounded in detail. The result has a general and a specific role of apology in relation to sacred architecture. It justifies the use of the classical orders, since their ultimate source was the Temple of Solomon: it was this divine architecture that came down to Vitruvius, along with the idea that the orders reflect human proportions. More specifically, it justifies the design of El Escorial and the extravagant ambitions of Phillip II for his spectacular palace.

In both volume two and three, Villalpando takes Ezekiel's description of the Temple, with its many detailed measurements, as the occasion for a mathematical

The Temple

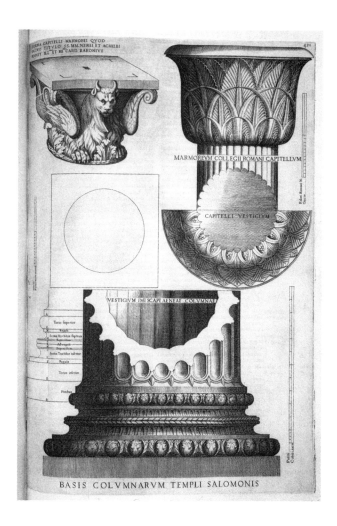

Figure 49
A comparison by Villalpando of capitals and column bases from various different sources. The scale accompanying the base of the column for the Temple of Solomon is in units of palms and cubits. Catalogue no. 51, p. 421.

treatise. The third volume, as well as dealing with the position of the Temple and the topography of Jerusalem, considers the ancient Hebrew weights and measures, since Ezekiel not only describes measurement with particular types and combinations of cubit, but was also instructed in the importance of 'just balances' and consistent standards of weight and of dry and liquid measure. As part of his comparative treatment of Hebrew, Greek and Roman measures, Villalpando announces the design of a mathematical instrument for determining the volumes of spheres and cubes and the weights of solid figures of different sizes.

Hartlib noted that there was a copy of this work in the Bodleian Library (*Hartlib Papers*, 29/3/8A [*Ephemerides*, 1635]). He later revealed his suspicion of

The Temple

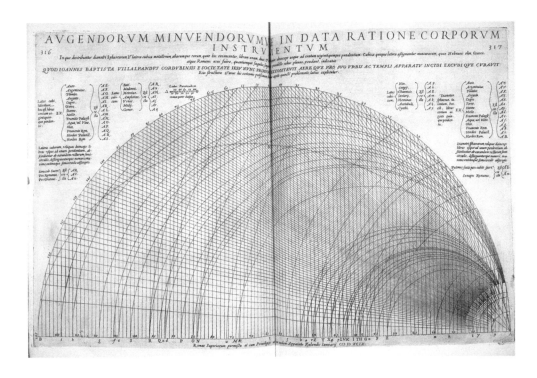

Figure 50
Villalpando's design for a mathematical instrument for determining the volumes of spheres and cubes and the weights of solid figures of different sizes.
Catalogue no. 51, pp. 316–7.

Jesuit mathematics in a note referring to Athanasius Kircher (catalogue nos. 37 and 46) and Galileo's opponent over sunspots, Christoph Scheiner (*Hartlib Papers*, 31/22/1A [*Ephemerides*, 1648]):

> Kircherus, Scheinerus etc apply Mathematics to Experiments and Mechanicks, etc. They are right Iesuits to make a great blaze of all things etc so as to attract more admirers and contributors to their Order.

G. Kubler, *Building the Escorial* (Princeton, 1982); J. A. Ramirez (ed.), *Dios arquitecto: J. B. Villalpando y el templo de Salomón* (Madrid, 1994); H. Rosenau, *Vision of the Temple: the Image of the Temple of Jerusalem in Judaism and Christianity* (London, 1979); R. Taylor, 'Architecture and Magic: Considerations on the Idea of the Escorial', in D. Fraser, H. Hibbard and M. J. Lewine (eds.), *Essays Presented to Rudolf Wittkower* (2 parts, London, 1967), part 1, pp. 81–109.

52. Matthias Hafenreffer
Templum Ezechielis
Tübingen, 1613
fol. in 6s:):(−3):(⁶ A−2G⁶
248 × 126 mm
I 1.11 Th. Seld.

Set beside that of the Jesuit Villalpando, this Lutheran commentary on Ezekiel raises similar questions but offers very different answers. Hafenreffer, who was Professor of Theology and Chancellor of the University of Tübingen, is more modest in the scope of his project and in his representation of the Temple. Like Villalpando, he is interested in its position, fabric, design, ornament and proportions. He also is led into a consideration of the Hebrew weights and measures, relating them to the standards of Wittenberg. Throughout he mixes geometry with spiritual commentary.

In an 'Appendix Geometrica', he says that the prophet has provided sufficient detail to discover the geometrical principles in the design of the Temple, evincing a sublime geometry of harmony and proportion, and in seeking to tease out this geometry, he has been in communication with two famous Protestant mathematicians and astronomers, Michael Maestlin and Johannes Kepler. He does not, however, share the mystical vision nor discover the grand correspondences of Villalpando.

H. Rosenau, *Vision of the Temple: the Image of the Temple of Jerusalem in Judaism and Christianity* (London, 1979).

53. Francis Bacon
New Atlantis. A Worke Vnfinished
Appended to: *Sylva Sylvarum: or a Natural Historie in Ten Centuries*
London, 1626
fol. in 4s: A–2N⁴ (*Sylva*); a–g⁴ (*New Atlantis*)
218 × 117 mm
Lister D 2

The utopian society Bacon described in his fable *New Atlantis* included a 'college' on the island of Bensalem called 'Salomon's House', where devout investigators worked on a collaborative, structured programme of experiment, collection and interpretation, aimed at extending natural knowledge and advancing its practical benefits, to 'the effecting of all things possible'. This was an influential vision and attempts were made to emulate Bacon's college in seventeenth-century England, such as by Samuel Hartlib and members of his circle. In 1654, the College of Physicians in London was declared by Walter Charleton to be 'Solomon's House in reality', while the Royal Society in London and the original Ashmolean Museum in Oxford can both be related to a similar inspiration. Each of these institutions included a collection displayed in a museum.

Bacon's college had been established by an ancient king called Solamona, who was remembered for his wisdom and for establishing the law. He had much in common with Solomon himself and named his foundation after, Bacon's visitors were told, 'the King of the Hebrewes, which is famous with you, and no Stranger to vs'. The appropriateness of this choice was even more clearly appreciated on Bensalem, where there survived 'some Parts of his works, which with you are lost, Namely that Naturall History, which hee wrote of all Plants, from the Cedar of Libanus, to the Mosse that groweth out of the Wall; And of all things that haue Life and Motion' (p. 19).

A. MacGregor, '"A Magazin of All Manner of Inventions": Museums in the Quest for "Salomon's House" in Seventeenth-Century England', *Journal of the History of Collections*, vol. 1 (1989), pp. 207–212 ; C. Webster, 'The College of Physicians: "Solomon's House" in Commonwealth England', *Bulletin of the History of Medicine*, vol. 41 (1967), pp. 393–412; C. Webster, *The Great Instauration* (London, 1975).

54. John Lightfoot
The Temple: Especially as it Stood in the Dayes of Our Saviour
London, 1650
4°: *⁴ A-2O⁴
153 × 93 mm
4° P 81 Th.

John Lightfoot was a noted biblical critic and Hebrew scholar. A Parliamentarian with Presbyterian views, he was appointed Master of St Catharine's Hall, Cambridge, by the Parliamentary Visitors in the year *The Temple* was published, and it was dedicated to William Lenthall, Speaker of the House of Commons. He played a considerable part in the preparation of the Polyglot Bible of 1657 (catalogue no. 73).

As his title states, Lightfoot was mainly concerned with Herod's Temple, though he does also deal with Solomon's and Zerubbabel's. He offers details on the dimensions and layout, comparing the height of the battlements, for example, with King's College Chapel in Cambridge. He is also interested in the contents of the Temple and the priestly practices. His treatise is a modest one and has no illustrations. Lightfoot tells his readers that he has drawn a large plan, which makes his description much easier to understand, but that he decided to publish his text first, 'to try what acceptance this treatise will finde, before I adde more paines and charge from the ingraving of the Map'.

The expense of copperplate engraving was a serious consideration. Hartlib noted in the year *The Temple* was published that: 'Dr Fuller is writing a Geography of Canaan with curious cuts which cost him 2. hundred lb. The worke may be called Speed's Canaan.' Lightfoot had links to this project also, as Hartlib records (*Hartlib Papers*, 28/1/52A [*Ephemerides*, 1650]):

> Hee [Fuller] and Lightfoot would make an excellent compound. The latter was purposing to write also vpon it as hee hath done of Temple-service, but then left it to Fuller who is no Antiquary but of stupendous witt and memory.

Thomas Fuller's *Pisgah-Sight of Palestine* was also published in 1650.

55. Samuel Lee

Orbis miraculum; or, the Temple of Solomon Pourtrayed by Scripture-Light
London, 1659
fol: A–5D²
218 × 113 mm
AA 61 Art.

Samuel Lee was a notable Puritan divine who was close to John Wilkins (see catalogue nos. 19, 36 and 43). After studying at Magdalen Hall, Oxford, he was created M. A. by the Parliamentary Visitors in April 1648, the same month as they appointed Wilkins Warden of Wadham. In October Lee was elected to a fellowship at Wadham, and he remained there despite a subsequent election to All Souls, becoming Sub-warden of Wadham in 1652 and Dean in 1653. He resigned his fellowship in 1657, Cromwell having appointed him minister of St Botolph's, Bishopsgate, in 1655. Under Wilkins, Wadham was a centre of activity in experimental natural philosophy. Lee dedicated his *Orbis miraculum* to the Warden, Fellows and Students: 'It was not long since my happiness and honour ... to enjoy a Fellowship for several years in that your goodly Seminary of all polite Literature.'

Lee has great respect for the editors of the Polyglot Bible (catalogue no. 73), 'whereby not only our Country, but the very age is honoured' (sig. A2). Although Villalpando's Temple is illustrated there, Lee denies that it can be a true representation of Solomon's. Rather, he says, it was derived from the visionary temple of Ezekiel, which cannot ever have existed: it was simply too large for Mount Moriah, where Solomon's Temple was built. Villalpando may have been 'the most learned and laborious Temple student, that ever proceeded into publick light', but his reconstruction was impossible. What Ezekiel saw was not a material building but 'the Church of Christ, being the Gospel-Temple, whose great enlargement was signified by that vision' (sig. A2 verso). In fact the illustration of the Temple building in *Orbis miraculum* seems to be derived from Montano (see figure 47). The editor of the Antwerp Polyglot Bible provided Lee with a more secure and rational model of the actual Temple, and his own modifications then take it in the direction of an English church.

In his first chapter Lee sets himself to establish the distance and direction between London and Jerusalem, and in doing so shows a reasonable familiarity with practical mathematics, appropriate to a tract addressed to Wilkins from an author present in Wadham during the 1650s. Values given by Ptolemy and by Selden are suppressed in favour of latitudes from Kepler's *Rudolphine Tables* and a longitude difference from Longomontanus. A more difficult question is the proper authority for the length of a degree. Historical re-assessments of the

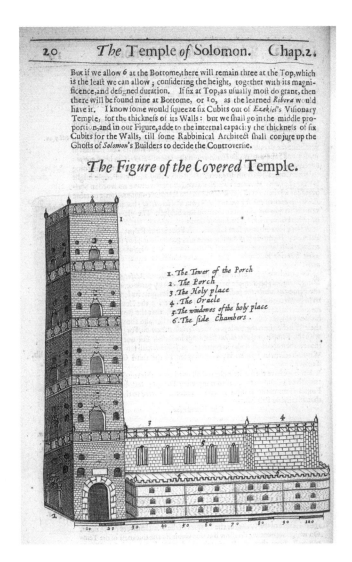

Figure 51

A very English interpretation for the design of Solomon's Temple, by an English author, the Puritan divine Samuel Lee. Lee argued that the extremely elaborate Temple designs of earlier authors took their inspiration from the visionary temple of Ezekiel, which was never intended as a real temple to be built on earth. What was required was a more practicable plan, which he thus provided. Catalogue no. 55, p. 20.

value given by Ptolemy are traced through Snell and Clavius, but 'to proceed to more certainty' Lee cites Gassendi and particularly *The Seaman's Practice* of Richard Norwood – 'a late learned Improver of his Mathematicall Knowledge towards the advancement of the Art of Navigation' (p. 10). Norwood's value was based on a survey he conducted between London and York in 1635. His work and his call for an improved determination led Lee into a discussion of the state of practical mathematics in England: 'our Observations and Experiments are now come to a greater maturity, for the encouragement of so worthy a Work' (p. 11). He refers to the advantages offered by the invention of

The Temple

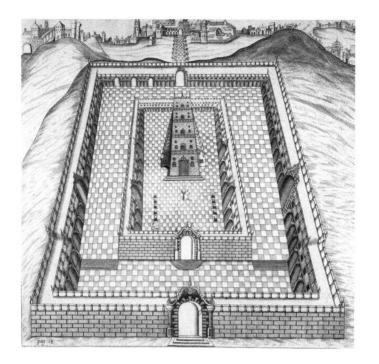

Figure 52 (Left)
Samuel Lee's covered temple building positioned at the centre of a double courtyard, itself sited within the confined space on top of Mount Moriah. Catalogue no. 55, plate facing p. 15.

Figure 53 (Right)
Jacob Judah Leon's plan of the camp of the Israelites during their wanderings. The Tabernacle of Moses (a tented precursor to the Temple of Solomon) is placed centrally. Catalogue no. 56, plate between pp. 28 and 29.

logarithms, and to the opinions of Vincent Wing and of William Oughtred, 'the incomparably learned in the Mathematicks ... the great Ornament of our Nation'. Determining the compass direction occasions further excursions into the English literature on practical navigation.

As for the Temple itself, it offers spiritual lessons about the gospel and the new covenant and Lee's substantial account of the building is a necessary preface to these, but he cannot attribute mystical significance to the design and dimensions. He discusses the cubit in some detail, but his treatment is sardonic and inconclusive. His description of the design is prosaic and matter-of-fact; it purposely distances the author from commentators 'who delight much to converse with numbers in the School of Pythagoras' (p. 181). Here Lee's attitude is in accord with that of his colleagues in Wadham, Wilkins and Seth Ward, as expressed in their *Vindiciae Academiarum* of 1654. We can take it that Lee's response to Villalpando was agreeable to Wilkins. It is also in line with the attitude of Christopher Wren (catalogue no. 60), who would have known Lee at Wadham.

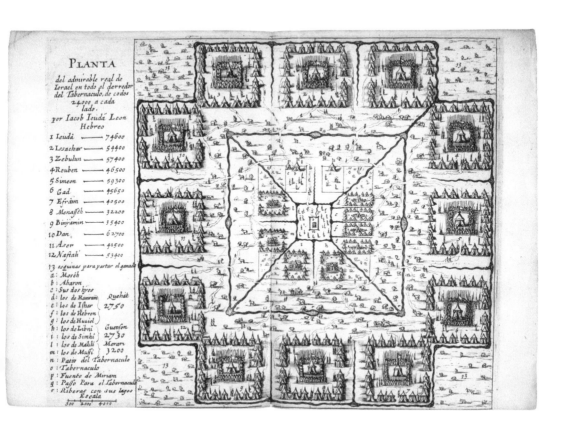

56. Jacob Judah Leon
Retrato del tabernaculo de Moseh
Amsterdam, 1654
4°: π *⁴ 2*² A–L⁴
177 × 135 mm
Opp. adds. 4° IV 487

Jacob Judah Leon was a rabbi and Sephardic scholar in Middelburg in Zeeland and later in Amsterdam. He became famous for his model of the Temple (catalogue no. 57), but he also made a model of its tented precursor, the Tabernacle of Moses. The description was first published in Dutch in 1647; the volume here is a Spanish edition with fine illustrations. Leon deals with the design and construction of the Tabernacle and its priestly management, as well as the camp of the Israelites in their wandering journey led by Moses. The model of the Tabernacle was an added attraction in the successful commercial exhibition of Leon's Temple.

The Temple

57. Jacob Judah Leon
De templo Hierosolymitano ... libri IV
Helmstadt, 1665
4°: a–c⁴):(⁴ A–2C⁴ 2D²
155 × 109 mm
4° R 81(1) Th.

Leon (see previous entry) was so associated in the public mind with his model of the Temple that he was given the name 'Templo'. The model was displayed with great success in Amsterdam, while his book was translated and published in eight languages. This edition is a Latin translation of 1665 by Johannes Saubertus, with fine plates. It is a straightforward account of the Temple and its contents, and of the nearby Palace of Solomon and the Antonia Tower, and could equally well serve as a description of the model.

John Dury wrote to Samuel Hartlib in 1646, in connection with their interest in the Dutch Hebrew scholar Adam Boreel, that Boreel had been studying the Jewish Mishnah with Leon. Leon was identified as the builder of the model of the Temple, which Dury had seen in the Netherlands, judging that 'amongst all the Rarities & Antiquities which are to bee taken notice of there is none to bee compared thereunto' (*Hartlib Papers*, 3/3/32A–33B).

Leon's models of the Temple and the Tabernacle were brought to London in the mid-1670s, and an English summary of both descriptions, dedicated to Charles II, was published in Amsterdam in 1675. Constantijn Huygens provided Leon with a letter of introduction to Christopher Wren, who would be able to judge the models and introduce Leon to the circle of the Royal Society. Whatever the motive for this move, whether connected with mathematical interest in the Temple or with millenarian aspirations that necessitated its reconstruction, they were overtaken by Leon's death in July 1675. However, it seems likely that it was in this connection that Robert Hooke recorded early in September, 'With Sir Chr. Wren. Long Discourse with him about the module of the Temple at Jerusalem' (Robinson and Adams, p. 179).

The Temple

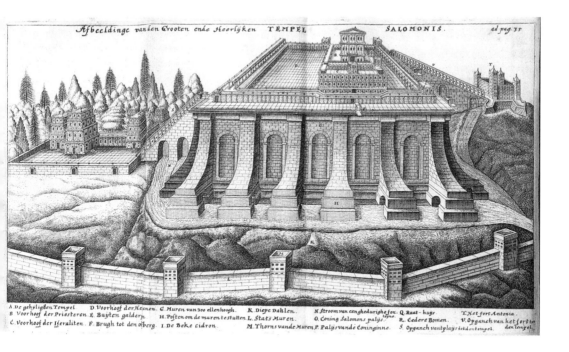

Figure 54
Engraving from an edition of Jacob Judah Leon's *De templo Hierosolymitano*. Leon achieved considerable fame in the mid-seventeenth century through his three-dimensional model of the Temple which was exhibited in Amsterdam; so much so that he himself was referred to as 'Templo'. Catalogue no. 57, plate facing p. 35.

A. K. Offenberg, 'Jacob Jehuda Leon (1602–1675) and his Model of the Temple', in J. van den Berg and E. G. E. van der Wall (eds.), *Jewish-Christian Relations in the Seventeenth Century* (Dordrecht, 1988), pp. 95–115; R. H. Popkin, 'Some Aspects of Jewish-Christian Theological Interchanges in Holland and England 1640–1700', in van den Berg and van der Wall, *op. cit.*, pp. 3–32; C. Provoyeur, *Le Temple: Représentations de l'architecture sacrée* (Nice, 1982); H. W. Robinson and W. Adams (eds.), *The Diary of Robert Hooke, 1672–1680* (London, 1935).

151

The Temple

58. Richard Cumberland
An Essay Towards the Recovery of the Jewish Measures and Weights
London, 1699
8°: A-F⁸
136 × 68 mm
Antiq. e.E. 1699.2

This is the second edition of Cumberland's *Essay*, the first having appeared in 1686; between the publications of the two editions the author had been appointed Bishop of Peterborough. Cumberland dedicates his tract to Samuel Pepys, President of the Royal Society, whom he had known since their student days at Magdalene College, Cambridge. He places his work on the recovery of ancient measures within the programme for 'the Improvement of Natural Knowledge, for which the Royal Society was founded' (sig. A2).

Cumberland points to the importance of measures in the Old Testament – the careful recital of them in relation to Noah's Ark, the Tabernacle, the Ark of the Covenant, the Temples of Solomon and Ezekiel and their sacred contents and utensils. These were 'the most ancient, beautiful, and magnificent proportions of Architecture to be recorded' (p. 2), and their designs, due to God himself, had been given in round numbers. The most holy place in Solomon's Temple, the inner sanctuary containing the Ark of the Covenant, was a perfect cube of 20 cubits.

Not only were the priests responsible for maintaining and administering standards of weight and measure, but when Ezekiel prophesied the restoration of religion and society almost a thousand years after Moses, he stipulated a return to the ancient cubit, ephah, shekel and gerah. The ancient measures derived from Noah and descended through his sons to the Egyptians, as well as to the Canaanites and Abraham. They were used by Joseph when he was in authority in Egypt and by Moses when writing the Pentateuch. They were embodied in the sacred utensils of the Temple.

Having determined the length of the cubit (almost 22 inches) and the measures of volume and weight in relation to this, Cumberland then seeks to make these results available to all nations by expressing the cubit in the universal measure of the length of a seconds pendulum (*cf.* Wilkins, catalogue no. 36). This is the 'Horary Yard' and 'Horary Foot', authority for which he derives from Christian Huygens's *Horologium oscillatorium* (Paris, 1673).

The relevance of this work to the Royal Society derives from the importance of standards of measure for settled community and Godly governance, while

The Temple

Figure 55
Richard Cumberland's illustration of a shekel next to the scale of a cubit, from his work on Jewish measures and weights. The units of measure laid out in the Old Testament were possible candidates for the 'universal measure' being sought at the end of the 17th century, since they were specified by God himself.
Catalogue no. 58, plate facing p. 1.

mankind's 'best Sciences' and 'most perfect Arts' are 'founded in the Principles of Numeration, and Mensuration, and built up by a close order and coherence of Demonstrations, such as no where else are to be found' (p. 133). The divine significance of such standards is demonstrated by the priestly office of their regulation, by their embodiment in sacred objects, and by their prominence in 'the Magnificence, Symmetry, and Beauty that was in the Structure of the Temple' (p. 130).

153

The Temple

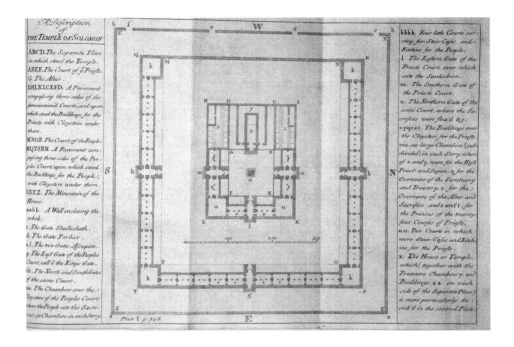

59. Isaac Newton
The Chronology of Ancient Kingdoms Amended
London, 1728
4°: A⁴ a⁴ A–3B⁴ A–D⁴ E² B–F² (with 3 engraved plates)
156 × 100 mm
CC 54 Art.

Between his account of the empires of the Babylonians and the Medes, and that of the Persians, Newton inserts 'A Description of the Temple of Solomon', offering no further justification than the observation that, since the Temple was destroyed by the Babylonians, a description 'may not be thought amiss' (p. 332). In fact he adds little to the subject, but his interest is worth acknowledging, if for no other reason, than to illustrate the currency of such questions even among some of the leading mathematicians of the seventeenth century.

The cubit Newton adopts is the 'sacred cubit', one of the alternatives familiar to the different writers on the Temple. It was longer than the common cubit by a hand's breadth, and Newton takes its length as between 21½ and 22 English inches. He gives a rather matter-of-fact description, while his principal source is Ezekiel's vision recorded in Hebrew and in Greek, working from the contemporary Hebrew and the Septuagint. His three engraved plates are in plan only and one includes a scale of sacred cubits.

Figure 56 (Left)
Diagram by Isaac Newton of the Temple of Solomon.
There could scarcely be a clearer demonstration of the significance of the Temple and other Biblical themes to the pursuit of natural knowledge in the seventeenth century than that provided by its most famous proponent, Newton.
Catalogue no. 59, p. 346.

60. Christopher Wren
Parentalia: or, Memoirs of the Family of the Wrens
London, 1750
fol: π^4 (a) a–c^2 B–2R^2 a–3a^2
257 × 142 mm
D 9.1 Art.

Several of Christopher Wren's tracts on architecture, included by his son Christopher in the *Parentalia*, are concerned with ancient buildings, but they show scant regard for either Pythagorean harmonies or the sacred principles employed by God as designer. Wren is interested in Solomon's Temple (see also catalogue no. 57), as he was in a number of ancient structures, but for him its status as architecture is not enhanced by its divine inspiration. Since Solomon employed Phoenician workmen and was in correspondence with King Hiram, he argues, what we might discover about the Tyrian style would enrich our knowledge of the Temple, but while the Bible gives us general dimensions, we have little knowledge of the architecture that was used. What we can be sure of, however, is that the 'fine romantick Piece, after the Corinthian Order' elaborated by Villalpando is 'mere Fancy' (p. 360). Pillars used in such early buildings were grosser even than the Doric order, and it is with evident preference that Wren turns to deal with the Ionic temple of Diana at Ephesus. His judgement of the buildings he considers has scarcely any devotional content and thus the hierarchy of designs he adopts is completely opposed to that of Kircher (catalogue no. 37). It is in keeping with his attitude to Villalpando that Wren rejects the Vitruvian association of the orders with human proportions: columns, he thinks, are more like trees than like men.

Figure 57
Woodcut of a 45-inch sheaf of barley, demonstrating the amazing powers of soap-ash as a fertilizer. Improvement in the yield of crops was a typical concern of Hartlib's circle of correspondents.
Catalogue no. 54, title-page verso.

HARTLIB CIRCLE

It is difficult to define the Hartlib circle precisely. The Hartlib circle was not a society with a membership that gathered regularly, but a more diffuse group of individuals, widely dispersed geographically. From the late 1620s to the early 1660s, hundreds of different people met or corresponded with Samuel Hartlib in order to discuss points of educational theory, divinity or natural philosophy, and to suggest schemes for practical improvement. Hartlib was assiduous in seeking out new contacts and informants, often through intermediaries. Much of the work which he recorded was done by individuals whom he never met and similarly Hartlib's own reputation was spread by publication and correspondence well beyond the circle of his immediate friends and acquaintances.

The limited selection of published books and pamphlets represented here cannot capture the full variety of Hartlib's friends and correspondents, or of their activities. What it does illustrate, however, is the broader discussion taking place within the Hartlib circle around the theme of improvement. Such discussion was often inspired by scripture, and branched out to include political and religious as well as practical matters. The authors or editors of the books and pamphlets represented also played an important role in some part of Hartlib's career and helped him to develop his ideas about nature and society, benefiting in turn from his intellectual and, in some cases, practical assistance. Works by other members of the Hartlib circle can be found in the other sections of the catalogue.

61. Gabriel Plattes
A Discovery of Infinite Treasure
London, 1639
4°: A⁴ a⁴ B–O⁴ P⁶
162 × 90 mm
Wood 496 (1)

Gabriel Plattes (d. 1644) was one of the first projectors whose work was taken up by Hartlib, in the late 1630s. He had originally been patronized by the inventor and drainage engineer, William Engelbert, and, with Hartlib's encouragement, he published on husbandry and mining, and carried out alchemical work. In 1641, his anonymous pamphlet, *A Description of the Famous Kingdome of Macaria*, set out a vision of a technological utopia, which he hoped the Long Parliament would pursue.

Plattes' writings combined practical knowledge and achievement with an interest in improvement. In *A Discovery of Infinite Treasure*, he proposed a number of remedies for current faults in English husbandry, some of which anticipated the suggestions of the agricultural improvers of the 1650s, or were amplified by them. He advocated the creation of a 'Colledge for Inventions in Husbandrie' (p. 72), which would ensure that advances in practice were applied to the public good, and described the operation of a seed-drill which he had invented. Both Plattes and Hartlib argued that, once land and labour were sensibly managed, England contained sufficient wealth and resources to provide amply for its people. Plattes maintained his confidence in this belief despite his own personal circumstances. Although he was supported by Hartlib, Cressy Dymock reported that Plattes was 'suffered to fall down dead in the streets for want of food'.

G. E. Fussell, *The Old English Farming Books from Fitzherbert to Tull 1523–1730* (London, 1947), p. 38; Charles Webster, 'The Authorship and Significance of "Macaria"', in Charles Webster (ed.), *The Intellectual Revolution of the Seventeenth Century* (London, 1974), pp. 369–85.

Figure 58
Cressy Dymock's plan for the division of a fenland plot. The scheme aimed to rationalize the arrangement of land under cultivation. From catalogue no. 62.

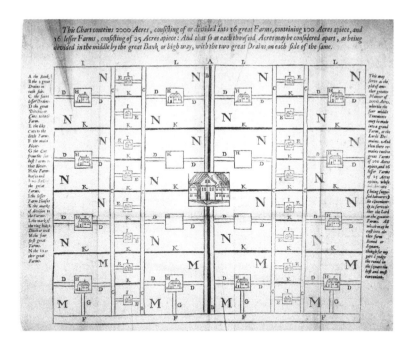

62. Samuel Hartlib (ed.)
A Discoverie for Division or Setting Out of Land
London, 1653
4°: A³ B-E⁴ F¹
147 × 93 mm
Vet. A3 e. 1252

In 1653, Hartlib published a letter from Cressy Dymock, an inventor and Nottinghamshire farmer, which reported on farming arrangements in the newly-drained Axholme fen. Dymock suggested several schemes for organizing farms on fenland in order to minimize transport costs, and to maximize the area under effective cultivation. Two of these were illustrated, in cuts based on Dymock's own drawings. The first, which is shown above, described the efficient division of a plot of 2,000 acres into 32 farms; the second explained the concentric division of a circular plot of 300 acres. Dymock shared Hartlib's concern for the improvement of agriculture, and was one of the proponents of a College of good husbandry, as well as of new techniques of sowing and manuring. He claimed to have perfected Plattes' engine for setting corn, and carried out a series of experiments on the relative yields produced by different methods of farming.

Richard Grove, 'Cressey Dymock and the Draining of the Fens: An Early Agricultural Model', *Geographical Journal*, vol. 147 (1981), pp. 27–37; *Hartlib Papers*, 62/29/1A-4B.

63. Gerard Boate
Irelands Naturall History
London, 1652
8°: A–N⁸
132 × 73 mm
8° E 7(3) Th. BS.

Gerard Boate (1604–1650) and his elder brother, Arnold (see catalogue no. 79) were both physicians who were educated at Leiden. Arnold Boate was also a noted Hebraist, and was patronized by James Ussher, Archbishop of Armagh (see catalogue nos. 80 and 81), arriving in Dublin in 1636. In 1641, the Boates published an attack on Aristotelian philosophy. In 1644, Arnold Boate, who had been appointed physician to the army in Leinster, left Ireland for Paris, where he continued to live until his death. Gerard Boate was appointed physician to the army in Ireland in 1647, but only took up his post, together with that of doctor to the Dublin military hospital, in 1649. The Boates were acquainted with the young Robert Boyle, and with others interested in the improvement of Ireland, such as Benjamin Worsley. By the mid-1640s, they had also come into contact with Hartlib and Dury.

In 1645, Gerard Boate began to compile a natural history of Ireland (which he had yet to visit), prompted by information given to him by his brother and the tales of Irish Protestant refugees then resident in London. His aim was to encourage further Protestant settlement by drawing attention to the potential riches of the country, and to praise the English for their supposedly improving rule, which had been threatened by the Irish rebellion of 1641. The work was avowedly Baconian in character and presented an economic geography of the island which reflected the regional, religious, and political biases of Boate's Protestant settler informants, especially that of the Parsons family from County Offaly.

Gerard Boate died in January 1650, when his book was far from complete. At this point, Hartlib stepped in to bring the work to publication, with the assistance of Boate's brother, Arnold, and of other friends. *Irelands Natural History* was dedicated to Cromwell and to the Lord-Deputy, Fleetwood, to whom Dury addressed a polemical, religious preface, which promised the restoration of all knowledge and the opening of the 'Intellectuall Cabinets of Nature' (sig. A4) to those who avoided the sin of excess sensuality. Dury hoped that Cromwell and Fleetwood would encourage the Protestant resettlement of Ireland, and provide land there for the Bohemians and other exiles.

Hartlib continued to promote work on the natural history of Ireland following the publication of Boate's book, in particular through the material included in the *Legacie* (catalogue no. 10). However, the deaths of both Arnold Boate and Robert Child frustrated any plans for an enlarged version of *Irelands Natural History*. Nevertheless, for members of the Hartlib circle, Ireland continued to represent a land of opportunity, in which the legal and customary restrictions on improvement which hampered projectors in England did not apply. It was a place which therefore had great potential to be a new Eden.

T. C. Barnard, 'The Hartlib Circle and the Cult and Culture of Improvement in Ireland', in Mark Greengrass, Michael Leslie, and Timothy Raylor (eds.), *Samuel Hartlib and Universal Reformation* (Cambridge, 1994), pp. 281–97; Patricia Coughlan, 'Natural History and Historical Nature: The Project for a Natural History of Ireland', in Greengrass, Leslie, and Raylor (eds.), *op. cit.*, pp. 298–317; T. C. Barnard, *Cromwellian Ireland* (Oxford, 1975), pp. 214-6 & 234-7; Charles Webster, *The Great Instauration* (London, 1975), pp. 428–35; *Hartlib Papers*, 15/5/18A–23B, 28/1/13B, 28/2/16B, 57/5/2A, 62/45/1A–7B.

64. Sir Hugh Plat
The Jewel House of Art and Nature
London, 1653
4°: A–2G⁴
165 × 90 mm
Vet. A3 e. 1456

Like *The Garden of Eden* (catalogue no. 13), Plat's *Jewel House*, a book of secrets which included a variety of experiments in husbandry, was highly regarded by members of the Hartlib circle. It was originally published in 1594. In 1653, a new edition was produced by Arnold Boate, with a dedication to Bulstrode Whitelocke and an additional discourse on stones (pp. 217–32), probably written by Boate himself. Among the agricultural achievements reported by Plat was the use of soap-ash as a fertilizer. Plat claimed that this had promoted the growth of massive sheaves of barley, some 45 inches long, at a farm in Middlesex in 1594. He illustrated this claim with a woodcut of a huge ear of barley, printed on the verso of the title-page (see figure 57, p. 156). Plat was particularly concerned with the correct method for planting and growing corn, and, in his *New and Admirable Arte of Setting of Corne* of 1600, he described a spade designed for this purpose as 'Adams toole revived'.

Bent Juel-Jensen, 'Some Uncollected Authors XIX: Sir Hugh Plat ?1552–?1611', *The Book Collector*, vol. 8 (1959), pp. 60–8; Blanche Henrey, *British Botanical and Horticultural Literature Before 1800* (3 vols, London, 1975), vol. 1, p. 155.

65. Samuel Hartlib (ed.)
The Reformed Common-Wealth of Bees
London, 1655
4°: A² B-I⁴
153 × 98 mm
4° H 4 (2) Art. BS.

During the early 1650s, one of the projects for improvement which interested many of Hartlib's correspondents was the promotion of beekeeping. Inspired by the profits reported by West Indian planters, who had recently begun to cultivate cane sugar, Hartlib and his friends, including members of the Council of Trade, looked for ways 'to turne England into Barbados' (as Benjamin Worsley put it, *Hartlib Papers*, 28/2/2B [*Ephemerides*, 1651]). Hartlib hoped that, by encouraging beekeeping, it would be possible to produce cheaper and more plentiful honey, which could substitute for expensive sugar, as well as being used as a food and in brewing. Consequently, he consulted his correspondents for information about bees and their habits, drawing on a wide range of contacts both in England and on the Continent.

In 1655, Hartlib published the results of his enquiries, in *The Reformed Common-Wealth of Bees*. This work included a contribution from Arnold Boate, on the generation of bees, as well as pieces by other members of the Hartlib circle. In particular, it printed several letters detailing new designs of beehive, of which the most striking was the transparent beehive developed by William Mewe, a Gloucestershire clergyman, following a model mentioned in Pliny. Mewe's invention had been further modified by John Wilkins and his young protégé, Christopher Wren (see catalogue nos. 18 and 60). Hartlib illustrated Wren's design, executed in May 1654, for a three-storey, transparent beehive (shown opposite). The bees were able to move between the various layers of the hive, and glass panels set into the structure allowed an observer to see the honey cascading down inside it. Although Wren's construction had not been an immediate success (due to a failure to realise that bees worked downwards), it offered the prospect of an ever-increasing stock of bees and honey within the same hive. Sir Cheney Culpeper was enthusiastic about the possibilities of transparent hives, 'wherein the whole waye of woorkinge of that little creature might be seene; by which wee might (I am confidente) haue vnsophisticated wines of our owne, cheaper & better then from other nations' (Braddick and Greengrass, p. 363).

Hartlib hoped that *The Reformed Common-Wealth of Bees* and the beehives which he promoted would receive official patronage, and he planned to present them to members of the Committee for Trade and Foreign Affairs. However, his schemes for increased production, and for the replacement of sugar with

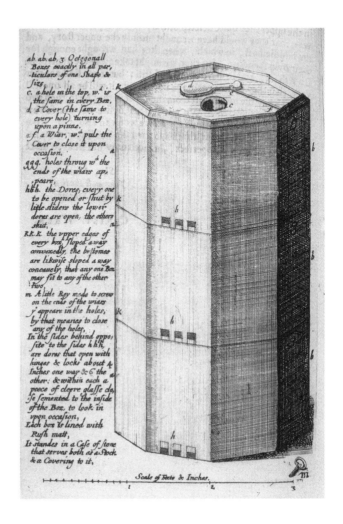

Figure 59
A three-storey beehive to the design of Christopher Wren. Inspired by a transparent hive mentioned in Pliny, this design had a number of glass observation panels through which an observer could watch the movement of honey inside. Catalogue no. 65, p. 52.

English honey and wine with mead, came to very little. Nevertheless, there remained lessons to be learned from the bees. Hartlib's interest in them had never been purely economic, since the ordered activity of the hive provided a model of pious industry and good husbandry. Through the activities of virtuous improvers, this, at least, might be replicated in the human commonwealth.

G. E. Fussell, *The Old English Farming Books from Fitzherbert to Tull 1523–1730* (London, 1947), p. 47; Timothy Raylor, 'Samuel Hartlib and the Commonwealth of Bees', in Michael Leslie and Timothy Raylor (eds.), *Culture and Cultivation in Early Modern England* (Leicester, 1992), pp. 91-129; M. J. Braddick and Mark Greengrass (eds.), 'The Letters of Sir Cheney Culpeper, 1641-1657', pp. 105-402 in *Camden Miscellany XXXIII* (Camden Society, Fifth Series, vol. 7, 1996), p. 362-3; *Hartlib Papers*, 28/2/2B, 25/9/2A-2B, 33/1/23A-24B, 70/6/1A-2B.

66. John Dury
A Briefe Relation of That Which Hath Been Lately Attempted to Procure Ecclesiasticall Peace Amongst Protestants
London, 1641
4°: π² B-E⁴ F²
143 × 90 mm
B 23.7 (3) Linc.

John Dury (1596–1680) was one of Hartlib's closest friends and collaborators from the late 1620s to the 1660s. Like Hartlib, he was deeply interested in the reform of education and philosophy, and committed to the cause of religious union among Protestants. Both men saw these as linked pursuits, in which the resolution of mental errors would contribute to the promotion of ecclesiastical peace and harmony, and direct the energy of Protestants into overcoming Roman Catholic power. In their hands, Baconian and Comenian philosophy became a weapon in the broader European conflict of the Thirty Years War, and a tool by which God's people might achieve the overthrow of Antichrist.

The son of a Scottish minister, Dury had grown up in Leiden, and later served as chaplain to the English Company of Merchants at Elbing, where he may perhaps have encountered Hartlib for the first time. From 1628, when he first petitioned the Swedish king, Gustavus Adolphus, Dury travelled extensively in central and northern Europe, seeking to unite the various Protestant denominations in order to oppose the Catholic powers more effectively. His attempts to reconcile religious differences, in particular those between the Lutheran and Reformed Churches, were largely unsuccessful, although they did receive the support of a number of prominent churchmen, including several English bishops. In order to maintain support for Dury's activities, Hartlib published an account of his travels and negotiations in 1641. This was addressed to the Long Parliament, in an attempt to win its aid and to encourage it to follow policies which might lead to evangelical union. It was also intended to clear Dury from the taint of Laudianism, and to demonstrate his commitment to the Protestant cause at a time when some Englishmen were tempted to interpret irenicism as a cover for Catholic plotting.

G. H. Turnbull, *Hartlib, Dury and Comenius* (Liverpool, 1947), pp. 127–222; Anthony Milton, '"The Unchanged Peacemaker"? John Dury and the Politics of Irenicism in England, 1628–1643', in Mark Greengrass, Michael Leslie, and Timothy Raylor (eds.), *Samuel Hartlib and Universal Reformation* (Cambridge, 1994), pp. 95–117; Bodleian Library, Ms. Rawlinson C 911, fols. 225–519; *Hartlib Papers*, 18/17/1A–3B.

67. John Dury
The Reformed Librarie-Keeper
London, 1650
12°: A–C¹²
98 × 56 mm
8° A 150 Linc.

One of the ways in which both Dury and Hartlib wished to promote educational reform and further knowledge was by exploiting the facilities of public libraries in London, Oxford, and Cambridge more efficiently. Dury expressed the hope that the work of the librarian might be as 'a factor and trader for helpes to learning, a treasurer to keep them and a dispenser to apply them to use, or to see them well used, or at least not abused' (Turnbull, p. 257). *The Reformed Librarie-Keeper* printed various proposals for the organization and use of libraries, which Dury had originally advanced in 1646. It was published together with Dury's plans for a reformed school in 1650. In that year, Dury was appointed keeper of the library of St James's Palace (formerly the King's Library), which was in a state of disorder. He installed new bookcases and urged that the trustees for the selling of the late king's goods should draw up an inventory of the books and medals, both measures being intended to make the library usable to the public. A few years later, Dury and Henry Langley unsuccessfully proposed Hartlib for the post of Bodley's Librarian.

As storehouses of learning, in which great strides had already been made to establish accurate classifications, libraries had the potential to be ideal embodiments of the Ark. But the poorly-funded libraries of interregnum England were too chaotic in organization and too inaccessible for ordinary readers to be able to fulfil the role in which Dury and Hartlib had cast them.

G. H. Turnbull, *Hartlib, Dury and Comenius* (Liverpool, 1947), pp. 257–70; Jane Roberts, 'The Limnings, Drawings and Prints in Charles I's Collection', pp. 115–29 in Arthur MacGregor (ed.), *The Late King's Goods* (London, 1989), p. 123; *Hartlib Papers*, 3/3/24A–25B, 3/3/30A–31B.

68. John Milton
Paradise Lost
London, 1668
4°: A⁴ a⁴ A–2T⁴ 2V²
165 × 105 mm
Douce MM 459

John Milton (1608–74) was a pupil of Joseph Mede, who was also an early influence on Samuel Hartlib in the 1620s. Hartlib and Milton collaborated on several fronts during the 1640s, sharing an interest above all in the reform of education. In 1644, Milton offered to write up his thoughts on this subject for Hartlib, who duly had them published. Although he remained wedded to a more humanist, less vocational style of instruction than some of Hartlib's other correspondents, he was committed, like them, to the idea of state support for education. During the 1650s, Milton served as Latin secretary to the Council of State, and maintained occasional contacts with Hartlib. Towards the end of that decade, he began to compose his great poem, *Paradise Lost*, which dramatized the story of the Fall. The work was completed by the mid-1660s, and, in April 1667, Milton reached an agreement with a publisher, whereby he was paid £5 for the right to print the poem, with a further £5 to follow after the sale of the first edition of 1,300 copies (and to be paid again on the sales of two subsequent editions). Various changes were made to the title-page during the course of printing; the copy here represents the fourth state of the first edition of the work. By this point, Milton's poem was selling well, and further editions were soon called for.

Despite the many heterodox beliefs of its author, *Paradise Lost* succeeded in becoming both a model for English verse and a popular guide to the interpretation of the opening chapters of Genesis, whose story it dramatized. Quotations from the poem frequently embellished people's attempts to interpret or apply the Bible (as can be seen in catalogue no. 20). Milton was particularly successful in capturing the emotions of Adam and Eve, and, thus, in making the biblical narrative more immediate and more affecting to his readers.

William Riley Parker, *Milton: A Biography*, edited by Gordon Campbell (2 vols, Oxford, 1996), vol. 1, pp. 508–9, 595–605 and vol. 2, pp. 1108–1113; Charles Webster (ed.), *Samuel Hartlib and the Advancement of Learning* (Cambridge, 1970), pp. 41–3.

Figure 60
Opening of the first edition of John Milton's *Paradise Lost*. *Paradise Lost* sold very well from its publication in 1667, and became both a model of English verse and a popular aid to the interpretation of the first chapters of Genesis. Milton had collaborated with Hartlib during the 1640s, particularly in the area of educational reform. From catalogue no. 68.

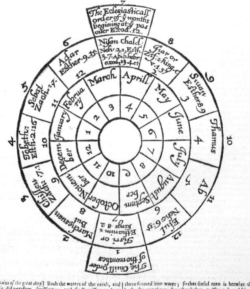

Figure 61

Diagram illustrating the order of the months, designed to facilitate calculation of the timing of 'the second month', mentioned in Genesis 7: 2 as the date of the beginning of the Flood.
Catalogue no. 71, sig. C2 recto.

BIBLICAL CRITICISM

Much seventeenth-century theology took the form of commentary on the text of scripture, which was generally believed to be the inspired word of God. For Protestants especially, the purpose was to bring out the literal meaning of the text, and to situate particular passages within the larger narrative framework of the Bible, often by providing doctrinal and historical context or by the use of cross-references. The Old and New Testaments were thought to constitute a single story, which was historically accurate and which taught clear lessons for moral practice. Exemplars drawn from the Bible provided models for contemporary human activity, in part by embodying types of ideal behaviour. Thus the figure of Solomon might be taken as the exemplar of the wise ruler, as he was in Bacon's writings (catalogue no. 53), and could be identified with a contemporary learned monarch, such as James I. Such typology could have controversial implications, for example in the rival characterizations of the Church of England as an ark of salvation and as the false idol, Dagon. Relatively few early modern readers of the Bible continued the medieval practice of a fourfold interpretation of scripture (literal, allegorical, tropological, and anagogical). They tended instead to favour more mystical, allegorical readings, often based on a complex typology, or more usually to rely on the elucidation of the apparent literal meaning of the text. Despite the philological elements introduced into the literal exegesis of scripture by humanist scholars, both of these early modern patterns of biblical interpretation grew out of the medieval scholastic tradition and owed much to it.

The early modern way of interpreting scripture was pre-critical in so far as it regarded the Bible as a special book whose message, although delivered in a particular historical context, transcended time. But it was not pre-critical in the sense of lacking method. In England, at least, individuals were encouraged to read the Bible in an attentive and ordered fashion, so as to preserve the narrative integrity of scripture and to be able to apply for themselves those parts of the Bible which spoke to humanity in general or which referred to specific times in the future. Preachers were taught to have regard for the context of the passages that they expounded. They were supposed to be sensitive to issues such as the time and place in which particular phrases had been uttered or words written. They were aware that certain parts of the Bible required special exegetical care, and that, in places, it might be necessary to desert the literal sense in order to bring out more important moral truths or defend the inspired word of scripture from the charge of absurdity. However, they also knew that such departures from normal critical practice should be sanctioned by reason, and, if possible, by the tradition of the early Christian Church.

The emphasis which the early Protestant reformers laid upon a personal encounter with the authentic words of scripture, combined with the value which humanist critics derived from a comparative and philological study of the text, encouraged many to acquire linguistic skills in Greek and Hebrew. These gave learned readers an immediate appreciation of the style of the Bible, albeit one which was sometimes stunted by the poverty of contemporary teaching, especially in oriental languages. Early modern critics were thus not unaware of changes in compositional techniques between different passages and books of the Bible, which were also brought out by the literal translations used by ordinary readers. However, they chose to interpret such material as conveying theological nuances or showing the accommodation of the divine message to particular historical contexts, rather than as a demonstration that the Bible had been composed by a number of different hands over time. On the contrary, the unity of the moral and theological message of the Bible helped to prove that it was the work of a single guiding principle, that of the Holy Ghost.

It was normally accepted among Protestants in the early modern period that the original text of the Bible had been preserved from change and harm by the action of providence. Despite this, new manuscript discoveries and the scrutiny generated by attempts to produce accurate, literal translations helped to channel the activities of many intellectuals into the field of textual scholarship. A number of different theories were developed about the history of the transmission of the text and about alterations which might have occurred to it over time (see catalogue nos. 73 to 78). In general, those who argued that the text had changed in some way also believed that it would be possible for Christian scholars to reconstruct the original, as it had been dictated by the Holy Ghost. There was a willingness to accept some human intervention in the editing and transmission of the Bible, but a general belief that this had been intended to preserve not to alter the original. If changes had occurred they were a product of the imperfect historical and linguistic knowledge of earlier editors which could increasingly be corrected as more information became available and skills improved. Such beliefs were consistent with contemporary doctrines of providence as well as with the history of linguistic and political change which had been derived from the Bible itself. They allowed space for textual and critical scholarship without threatening the central position of scripture within reformed religion.

Many critics ranged widely in order to understand the details of biblical history and to establish the exact contexts for customs and practices described in the Bible. Their work increasingly took in comparative materials, drawn from the study of past and contemporary Jewish and eastern religion, as well as applying the findings of textual and material scholarship. Astronomical data was applied to help verify the details of biblical chronology and to establish its true relationship to the secular chronologies of the ancient world. Anthropological and archaeological findings were deployed to try to generate an understanding of obscure practices described in the Bible, such as the true form of the worship of the Jewish Temple. Specifics which were derived from the results of such criticism might find their way in turn into the interpretation of prophetic texts, the understanding of whose mystical language depended on a detailed knowledge of the order of past events and the forms of biblical religion. The growing reliance of early modern critics on historical and natural evidences did not usually compromise their acceptance of the literal sense of scripture. On the contrary, the testimony of the natural world in the past, the present, and the future seemed to many to confirm truths about religion and providence which could be found expressed most clearly in the Bible.

However, such reliance on the literal sense of the Bible was not without its problems. In unskilled or untutored hands, the injunction to search the scriptures for oneself could lead to theological errors and to a worrying tendency to justify actions by reference to supposed biblical proofs, found in passages which were quoted out of their true contexts. It was also tempting to resort to allegory or to mystical readings of the Bible when the literal sense appeared obscure or unbelievable, rather than to puzzle over historical contexts or linguistic conundrums. After the Restoration, many orthodox divines, especially within the Church of England, stressed the difficulty of understanding the Bible and the need for assistance from a trained interpreter, such as a priest, when tackling certain kinds of reading. They did so in order to limit the spread of what seemed to them idiosyncratic and often dangerous or heretical interpretations of the Bible. But, in the process, they helped to create a more divided approach to understanding the text. The reformed principles of the perspicacity and sufficiency of scripture thus became more controversial.

Biblical Criticism

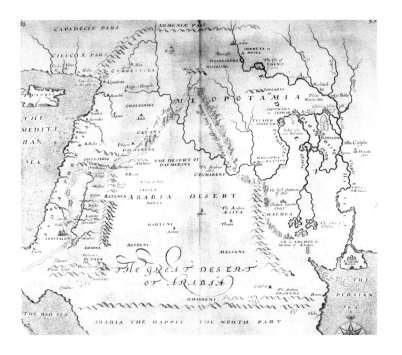

Figure 62 & 63
Walter Ralegh's maps of the location of paradise (left) and of the dispersion of peoples (opposite). Ralegh placed both the Garden of Eden and the Tower of Babel in Mesopotamia.
From catalogue no. 30, plates between pp. 56 & 57 and 152 & 153, respectively.

A growing awareness of problems associated with the text, and of the divergence between Jewish and Christian exegesis, helped to inspire more heterodox interpretations of the Bible from the time of the Reformation onwards (see catalogue no. 84). Some of these cast doubt on the authorship of scripture; others questioned its historicity. However, such interpretations tended to provoke controversy rather than inspire assent for most of the early modern period. The apparently overwhelming evidence of contemporary scholarship in history, comparative mythology, and natural philosophy seemed to Protestants to support their literal readings of the Bible and the belief that past and present were subject to providential guidance. To place too much stress on minor inconsistencies and doubts appeared in contrast to be evidence of a scepticism which bordered on atheism or of an acceptance of Catholic arguments in favour of the superiority of the teachings of tradition over the findings of reason and individual experience. For most Protestants, the theological as well as the scholarly motivation for continuing to value the literal sense of scripture was thus compelling.

David C. Steinmetz, 'The Superiority of Pre-Critical Exegesis', reprinted in Stephen E. Fowl (ed.), *The Theological Interpretation of Scripture* (Oxford, 1997), pp. 26–38; Richard A. Muller, 'Biblical Interpretation in the Era of the Reformation: The View from the Middle Ages', in Richard A. Muller and John L. Thompson (eds.), *Biblical Interpretation in the Era of the Reformation* (Grand Rapids, 1996), pp. 3–22; Patrick Collinson, 'The Coherence of the Text: How it Hangeth Together: The Bible in Reformation England', in W. P. Stephens (ed.), *The Bible, the Reformation and the Church* (Sheffield, 1995), pp. 84–108.

Biblical Criticism

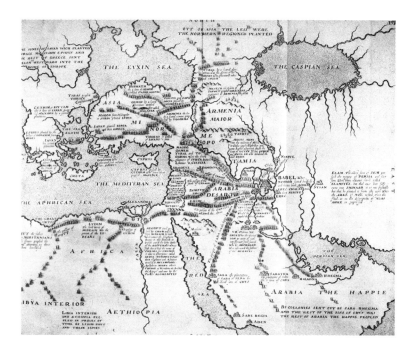

69. Maps from Walter Ralegh
The Historie of the World in Five Books
See catalogue no. 30

These maps from Ralegh's *Historie of the World in Five Books* (catalogue no. 30) show the situation of paradise, and the location of the Tower of Babel and the dispersion of peoples from it. They demonstrate the extent to which early modern readers of the Bible conceived of its stories as conveying geographical, historical, and ethnographical fact.

Several features of these maps are also notable in the context of catalogue numbers 46 to 50 and 83 to 86. Ralegh placed Eden in Babylonia, where the Tower of Babel was built. The map locating Babel clearly shows the dispersion of peoples, and indicates which modern races were eventually descended from the biblical patriarchs. Ralegh also equated Ararat with Taurus, a mountain in the Caucasus, and suggested that some of Shem's descendants (Ophir and Havilah) had set out for the east before Nimrod had settled in Shinar (see figure 26, p. 85). Unlike Verstegan (catalogue no. 48), Ralegh traced the ancestry of the inhabitants of England through the *Cimbri*, descendants of Gomer's son Javan, rather than of Ashkenaz. This was a common choice for the ancestry of the English during the seventeenth century, not least because it allowed the option of accepting the legend that Trojan exiles had been the first to people the country.

70. Henry Ainsworth
Annotations Upon the First Book of Moses, Called Genesis
[Amsterdam], 1616
4°: 3✳⁴ 3+² A-2K⁴
185 × 135 mm
Vet. B2 e. 24

Henry Ainsworth (1569–1622), was teacher and leader of the English separatist congregation at 'the Ancient Church' in Amsterdam. Educated at Caius College, Cambridge, he improved his Hebrew through contact with Dutch Jews. He was at the centre of a network of scholarly and controversial printing by English exiles in the Netherlands, relying particularly on the services of Giles Thorp, an elder in his congregation. Ainsworth was the author of a commentary on the Pentateuch (originally published between 1616 and 1619) which was widely respected for the skill of its oriental scholarship and for the tenacity with which it adhered to the literal meaning of the text.

Although some writers criticized Ainsworth for being too ready to follow the conclusions of Jewish authors and rabbinic scholarship, most were grateful for the information which he synthesized. Thus, Hartlib argued that 'Commentarii should bee written as Ainsworth explaining only the words phrases et sense', and he bemoaned the fact that Ainsworth had died before he 'had done all summaries upon the whole Bibel as hee hade done upon the 5. bookes of Moses' (*Hartlib Papers*, 29/3/13B [*Ephemerides*, 1635] and 29/2/3A [*Ephemerides*, 1634]). Interest in and regard for Ainsworth's work did not abate, despite the provision of new commentaries on the Bible during the 1640s and 1650s (see catalogue nos. 71 and 72). Ainsworth's *Annotations* were recommended as a foundation for the marginal notes which were intended to accompany the revision of the Authorized Version, planned by the Council of State in 1652, and entrusted to the care of a committee including Ralph Cudworth, a Cambridge divine and advocate of Hartlib's schemes for the reformation of learning. This committee expressed particular interest in Ainsworth's unpublished manuscripts.

Although the planned revision of the English Bible eventually came to nothing, the search for further material by Ainsworth continued. Thus, during the last couple of years of his life, Hartlib tried to organize Dury to locate Ainsworth's nachlass in the Netherlands. He was prompted in this endeavour by his friend, John Worthington (see catalogue nos. 1 and 3), who had been associated with the revision of the English Bible, and who praised Ainsworth's 'most exact observation of the proper idioms of the holy text', and considered that, of any surviving manuscripts, ones 'upon the Prophets, or the New Testament, they

Biblical Criticism

are most desirable' (*Diary and Correspondence*, vol. 1, pp. 264 and 353). However, Dury's efforts were ultimately unsuccessful, since Ainsworth's son did not consider that his father's reputation would be enhanced by the publication of his remaining manuscripts.

Keith L. Sprunger, *Trumpets from the Tower: English Puritan Printing in the Netherlands 1600–1640* (Leiden, 1994), pp. 62-5, 70-4, 84-98, 194-5; *Calendar of State Papers Domestic* (1652-3), p. 74; James Crossley (ed.), *The Diary and Correspondence of Dr. John Worthington* (2 vols. in 3 parts, Manchester, 1847-86, Chetham Society, vols. 13, 36 & 114), vol. 1, pp. 263, 264, 271, 276, 279, 308, 309, 317, 335, 345, 351, 353 and 365; *Hartlib Papers*, 4/4/29A-B, 29/2/3A, 29/3/13B.

71. Westminster Assembly of Divines
Annotations Upon All the Books of the Old and New Testament
2nd edition, 2 vols, London, 1651
fol. in 4s: A³ ¶³ A-2C⁴ 2D² 3A-3Z⁴ 3a-3d⁴ 3e² 4A-8H⁴ 8I² (vol. 1 only)
305 × 160 mm
Broxb. 50.2

One of the principal tasks of the Westminster Assembly of Divines, which met between 1643 and 1649, was to provide an authorized commentary on the scriptures to accompany the text of the English Bible which had been published in 1611. The notes of the Westminster Divines soon outgrew the margins for which they were intended, and thus had to be published separately. According to a note on the flyleaf of this copy, the annotations on Genesis were the work of John Ley (1583-1662), who had previously written in defence of the interpretations given in the margins of the Geneva Bible (see catalogue no. 4). Hartlib had petitioned the Westminster Assembly for support during the 1640s, and he seems to have approved of the work of the annotators.

James Reid, *Memoirs of the Wetminster Divines* (Paisley, 1811, reprinted Edinburgh, 1982), pp. 50-4; *Hartlib Papers*, 29/6/9A.

72. Theodore Haak (trans.)
The Dutch Annotations Upon the Whole Bible
2 vols, London, 1657
fol. in 4s: π² A¹ B⁶ B-3Z⁴ 3A-3M⁴ 3N¹ 4A-4N⁴ 4O¹
245 × 140 mm
S 9.7 Th. (vol. 1 only)

Among the works which the Westminster Divines had commended as being particularly useful for the interpretation of the Bible were the 'Dutch Annotations'. These had been produced by the committee that had overseen the translation of the Bible into Dutch, as authorized by the Synod of Dort in 1618. They were published with the Dutch Bible in 1637.

Theodore Haak (1605–90), a German émigré friend of Hartlib, who had previously served as an envoy to Denmark, won Parliamentary approval for a translation of the Dutch Annotations, and was granted copyright in the work for fourteen years from 1646. Haak's initial progress was slow, however, and in 1648 he was forced to start again from the beginning of the translation, following a new method. A major difficulty was the fact that the Dutch text to which the annotations referred did not always concur with the Authorized Version. Further diplomatic activity distracted Haak from his task in the early 1650s, but, after May 1655, he worked solidly at the *Annotations*, completing them in 1657. The result was a literal, word-for-word translation of the original, that, however, omitted some of its aids to interpretation, in particular four maps after which John Worthington later inquired. Haak's work provided English readers with a verse-by-verse, literal commentary on the text of the Bible, including, for example, a discussion of the true identity of the rivers mentioned in Genesis, chapter 2, an important aid in fixing the location of Eden.

Pamela R. Barnett, *Theodore Haak, F. R. S. (1605–1690)* (The Hague, 1962), pp. 71–5 & 114–19; *Journals of the House of Commons*, vol. 4 (1644–46), p. 735; James Crossley (ed.), *The Diary and Correspondence of Dr. John Worthington* (2 vols. in 3 parts, Manchester, 1847–86, Chetham Society, vols. 13, 36 & 114), vol. 1, pp. 324 & 342; David Laing (ed.), *The Letters and Journals of Robert Baillie* (3 vols, Edinburgh, 1841–42), vol. 2, p. 188, and vol. 3, pp. 7, 8 & 304; *Hartlib Papers*, 21/11/3A–4B.

73. Brian Walton (ed.)

Biblia sacra polyglotta
6 vols, London, 1653–57
fol: π² A⁴ B–C² D¹ A–N² O¹ A–2C² (prolegomena); A–5T² (Pentateuch)
376 × 230 mm
fol. BS. 208 (vol. 1 only)

Polyglot editions of the Bible were flagships of sixteenth and seventeenth-century humanist scholarship. Erudite works grounded on the collection, collation, and publication of manuscript texts of scripture in an increasingly ambitious and bewildering array of languages, they promised to provide the materials for an eventual reconstruction of the original, pure text of the Bible, as it had been dictated by the Holy Ghost, based on the comparison of the variant readings preserved in the different languages through which the tradition had been transmitted in antiquity. Over a period of more than two decades, scholars in Paris had worked to produce a grand Polyglot, which was eventually completed in 1645. Impressive though they were, the resulting volumes were prohibitively expensive (a set cost as much as £50), and failed to include the fruits of all the manuscript and linguistic traditions which had become available to western critics by the 1640s. As a result, the idea was raised in England of editing a new Polyglot, including fresh material (especially in Arabic, Samaritan, and Syriac) drawn from a wider and more accurate range of sources, which would be laid out in a more helpful fashion and made available at a more affordable price.

The London Polyglot was conceived by Brian Walton (1600–61), the former rector of St Martin's Orgar (see also catalogue nos. 75 and 77), who had been deprived in 1641 because of his introduction of Laudian ceremony and his disagreements with his parishioners over the payment of tithes. Resident again in London during the 1650s, Walton quickly won the backing of Archbishop Ussher and John Selden, and, in 1652, his project was given the approbation of the Council of State. In the following year, Walton and his agents were promised the right to import paper for the printing of the Polyglot without payment of duty. This was a significant concession which substantially reduced production costs and allowed the use of high-quality paper from the Auvergne for at least some of the work. The undertakers began to raise subscriptions for the printing of the Polyglot, promising to supply the entire book for a down-payment of £10.

The initial prospectus for Walton's Polyglot generated critical comment, not least from Arnold Boate (see catalogue no. 79), in part because of the poor quality of its Hebrew and Syriac type, and the resulting large number of errors which it contained. Nevertheless, by 1653, Walton had found a new printer, Thomas Roycroft, and had new oriental types cut for the printing of the Polyglot.

Biblical Criticism

Sufficient money had been raised to allow printing to begin in 1653 or 1654, when Walton delivered the first parts of the manuscript of the text of the Pentateuch. Walton had also assembled an impressive array of collaborators, who aided him in the production of the complex text of the Polyglot, where Arabic, Aramaic, Ethiopic, Greek, Hebrew, Latin, Persian, Samaritan, and Syriac versions of parts of the Bible jostled with one another, sometimes requiring the presentation of as many as eight variants of the same passage, side by side.

Over the four years between 1653 and 1657, Walton and his collaborators gathered manuscript readings from across Europe, and collated them into the successive parts of the Polyglot. The work was completed with exceptional speed, although (to the later surprise of Henry Oldenburg) Walton was frustrated in his attempt to include Coptic and Armenian materials by the failure of copies of manuscripts to arrive from Rome. The last volume of the Polyglot contained a battery of scholarly commentary and material by Walton's collaborators, and the editor himself added a series of lengthy prolegomena to the first volume, in which he published the findings of several Continental scholars, notably Louis Cappel (see catalogue no. 79). The prolegomena were illustrated with engravings by Wenceslaus Hollar, including some modelled on Villalpando's designs of the Temple (see catalogue no. 51).

Although there were problems in obtaining the promised grant for duty-free paper, which held up production and contributed to some delays in the distribution of copies to subscribers, and although the price had to be raised slightly to take account of extra material, the London Polyglot was a considerable success. There were those who were worried by the implications of its scholarship, but few questioned its accuracy and completeness, or the achievement in bringing it to press so quickly. Hartlib considered that the production of the Polyglot underlined the potential usefulness of government support for a standing learned press. Walton thanked Cromwell and the Council of State for their patronage in the original preface to the Polyglot, but always wished to dedicate the work to the exiled Charles II, which he was able to do in 1659. After the Restoration, in 1660, Walton was appointed Bishop of Chester. By then, the international reputation of his work was established, and foreign as well as English scholars were eager to purchase copies that remained for sale at prices which had risen to £17 or £18.

The first volume of the Polyglot, containing the Pentateuch, which was the first part to be printed, and the prolegomena, which were published last, was illustrated with an engraved portrait of the editor by Pierre Lombart (see figure 66, p. 184). It shows Walton at work, with the sources of the Polyglot and some of the major works of Continental scholarship on his shelves behind him. Facing the portrait was the title-page, engraved by Hollar according to a design

Figure 64
Title-page from the first volume of the London Polyglot Bible, edited by Brian Walton. The title-page was designed by John Webb and engraved by Wenceslaus Hollar. It is in the form of a triumphal arch, on which are depicted eight biblical scenes, including, at the top, the gift of tongues at Pentecost. From catalogue no. 73.

by John Webb. This is in the form of a triumphal arch, bearing illustrations of eight biblical scenes, including Adam and Eve, Noah and the Ark, several scenes from the life of Christ, and, in the centre of the design at the top, the gift of tongues at Pentecost. Both symbolically and literally, Walton's Polyglot reunited the languages which had been separated at Babel, and promised to achieve a new understanding of the message of the Holy Ghost through its mastery of the divided traditions of the biblical text.

T. H. Darlow and H. F. Moule, *Historical Catalogue of the Printed Editions of Holy Scripture* (2 vols, London, 1911), vol. 2, pp. 23–6; Henry John Todd (ed.), *Memorials of the Life and Writings of the Right Rev. Brian Walton, D. D.* (2 vols, London, 1821), vol. 1; G. J. Toomer, *Eastern Wisdome and Learning: The Study of Arabic in Seventeenth-Century England* (Oxford, 1996), pp. 202–10; John Bold, *John Webb* (Oxford, 1989, reprinted 1990), p. 38; Richard Parr (ed.), *The Life of the Most Reverend Father in God, James Usher* (London, 1686), pp. 588–90 & 605–6; David Laing (ed.), *The Letters and Journals of Robert Baillie* (3 vols, Edinburgh, 1841–42), vol. 2, p. 387 and vol. 3, pp. 24, 302–6, 309–10 & 401; *Calendar of State Papers Domestic* (1651–52) p. 328, (1653–54) pp. 16 & 428, (1655) pp. 234 & 351, (1655–56) pp. 161, 199–200, 285–6, 339 & 366, (1656–57) p. 355, (1657–58) pp. 19, 188 & 220; British Library, Ms. Add. 32093, fols. 308, 309, 333 & 335; British Library, Ms. Add. 34164, fol. 100; British Library, Ms. Lansdowne 1055, fols. 2, 4, 6, 13, 21, 40 & 44; Bodleian Library, Ms. Tanner 49, fol. 42; Bodleian Library, Ms. D'Orville 469, pp. 337–8, Ms. D'Orville 470, pp. 248–9; *Hartlib Papers*, 39/3/29A–30B, 47/8/10A–11B.

74. Johannes Buxtorf the elder
Tiberias sive commentarius Masorethicus
Basel, 1620
4°:):(⁴ 2):(⁴ A–2Q⁴ 2R²
163 × 99 mm
4° B 36 Art. Seld.

Johannes Buxtorf the elder (1564–1629) was professor of Hebrew at Basel, and one of the leading Protestant scholars of the early seventeenth century. He was particularly interested in the history of the transmission of the text of the Bible among the Jews, and was concerned to establish the history of Jewish doctrine and ceremonial law. Buxtorf drew his information in part from Jewish informants, but he remained, in general, hostile to their religion, which he interpreted as being fixated on outward forms, and shaped by a hatred of Christianity. Nevertheless he was responsible for raising the standards of Hebrew knowledge and education among Protestants, in part through his grammatical and lexicographical publications, which tried to present Semitic languages in ways which would be familiar to contemporary students of Latin.

Buxtorf's scholarly energies came to concentrate especially on the scriptural and exegetical traditions of the Jews around the time of Christ, and focussed on the Aramaic recensions and interpretations of the Bible which had been made then. He possessed a collection of important Aramaic manuscripts which were inherited by his son, also a Christian Hebraist, and later consulted by Walton (see catalogue no. 73) and others. Buxtorf used these in his most important work, the Basel edition of the rabbinic Bible. Both the elder and the younger Buxtorf were tireless defenders of the theory, advanced in *Tiberias*, that the vowel points of the Hebrew Bible were originally the work of Ezra and 'the Great Synagogue', and consequently that they were coeval with the language and composition of the inspired text of scripture.

Buxtorf traced a single tradition of text and language from the time of Ezra onwards, and argued that the post-Christian Masoretes had simply had an editorial role in the construction of the vocalized Hebrew Bible. This was a view which came into increasing dispute in the middle of the century, involving the Buxtorfs in considerable controversy with those who argued that the vowel points were in fact additions to the text, reflecting the language and understanding of later readers of the Hebrew Bible, long after its first composition. The position adopted by the two Buxtorfs was consistent with the Protestant desire to interpret the original texts of the Bible as being the inspired word of God, preserved in its entirety by the protection of providence. Because of their doctrinal reliance on the literal sense of scripture, many Protestants were reluctant to concede that the text and its meaning might have changed over time.

This copy of *Tiberias* belonged to the English statesman and orientalist, John Selden (1584-1654), who wrote extensively about rabbinic law and Jewish customs, and was involved in promoting the idea of the London Polyglot in the early 1650s. The title-page bears Selden's motto, 'περὶ παντὸς τὴν ἐλευθερίαν' ('[I value] liberty above all'). Selden bequeathed many of his manuscripts and oriental books to the Bodleian Library.

William Dunn Macray, *Annals of the Bodleian Library* (2nd edition, Oxford, 1890), pp. 110-23; Stephen G. Burnett, *From Christian Hebraism to Jewish Studies: Johannes Buxtorf (1564–1629) and Hebrew Learning in the Seventeenth Century* (Leiden, 1996); Frank E. Manuel, *The Broken Staff: Judaism through Christian Eyes* (Cambridge, Mass., 1992), pp. 82-92.

75. Brian Walton
Introductio ad lectionem linguarum orientalium
2nd edition, London, 1655
12°: A-G¹² H¹⁰
125 × 68 mm
Douce W 54

Walton's project for a Polyglot Bible (catalogue no. 73) met with some early criticism in 1653-4 because of fears that the variant texts which it presented would undermine belief in the authority of the Bible. Using material which was later incorporated into the prolegomena to the Polyglot, Walton replied to his critics in the first edition of the *Introductio*, published in 1654. He set out a method for understanding oriental languages, and outlined the uses to which the different surviving texts of the Bible could be put.

Walton stressed that there were really benefits to the multiplicity of versions, since they allowed one to construct the history of the transmission of the Bible, and to correct errors which had crept into the text over time, in particular those introduced by earlier editors, such as the Masoretes, who were unsympathetic to the true, Christian message. He argued that a knowledge of the full range of ancient, oriental texts of the Bible provided assistance in determining the true meaning of the original, since, following the confusion of languages at Babel, not even Hebrew had been completely preserved from the alterations of time. Although he maintained a humanist faith in the possibility of establishing the true, authoritative text of scripture, Walton was thus sensitive to the differences

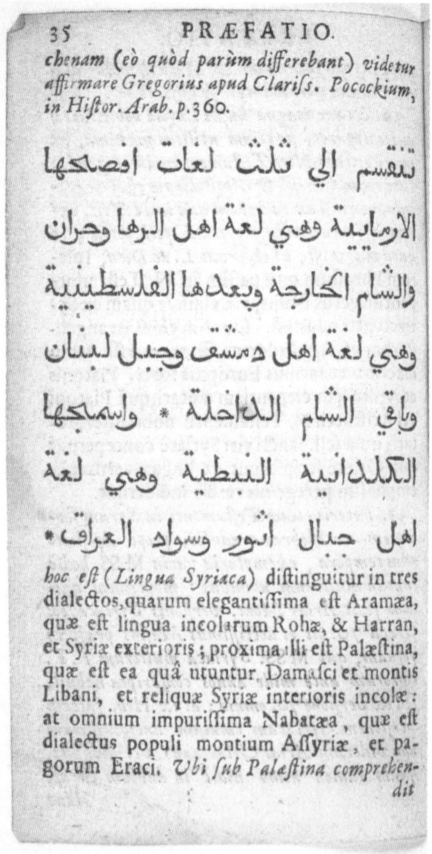
35 PRÆFATIO.
chenam (eò quòd parùm differebant) videtur affirmare Gregorius apud Clariſs. Pocockium, in Hiſtor. Arab. p. 360.

تنقسم الي ثلث لغات افصحها
الارمانية وهي لغة اهل الرها وحران
والشام الخارجة وبعدها الفلسطينية
وهي لغة اهل دمشق وجبل لبنان
وباقي الشام الداخلة * واسمجها
الكلدانية النبطية وهي لغة
اهل جبال اثور وسواد العراق *

hoc eſt (Lingua Syriaca) diſtinguitur in tres dialectos, quarum elegantiſſima eſt Aramæa, quæ eſt lingua incolarum Rohæ, & Harran, et Syriæ exterioris; proxima illi eſt Palæſtina, quæ eſt ea quâ utuntur Damaſci et montis Libani, et reliquæ Syriæ interioris incolæ: at omnium impuriſſima Nabatæa, quæ eſt dialectus populi montium Aſſyriæ, et pagorum Eraci. *Ubi ſub Palæſtina comprehendit*

Figure 65
A page from the preface of Brian Walton's *Introductio ad lectionem linguarum orientalium* open to a discussion of Syriac. Walton used the *Introductio* to respond to the critics of his Polyglot Bible and to justify the value of studying the text of scripture in ancient and oriental languages.
Catalogue no. 75, p. 35.

between versions. Also, as an Englishman who was proud of his country's recent acquisition of the *Codex Alexandrinus* (a manuscript of the Greek Old Testament), Walton was especially reluctant to concede automatic priority to the surviving Hebrew text of the Bible.

Henry John Todd (ed.), *Memorials of the Life and Writings of the Right Rev. Brian Walton, D. D.* (2 vols, London, 1821), vol. 1, pp. 68–71.

76. John Owen

Of the Divine Originall, Authority, Self-Evidencing Light, and Power of the Scriptures
Oxford, 1659
8°: *[8] A–Z[8]
122 × 73mm
Vet. A3 f. 1706

One of those who was disturbed by the implications of the London Polyglot (catalogue no. 73), and by Walton's defence of the work in both his *Introductio* and in the prolegomena to the Bible, was John Owen (1616–83). Owen was the leading minister among the congregationalists of the mid-seventeenth century and was appointed as Dean of Christ Church by the Parliamentarian Visitors of Oxford University. He was also closely involved in discussions about the revision of the English translation of the Bible which were going on in the 1650s, and deeply disturbed by contemporary expressions of heretical ideas about scripture, in particular those of the Socinians.

Owen believed that critics who denied the peculiar perfection of scripture were agents of 'the Synagogue of *Rome*' (sig. *2 verso), who cast doubt on the clarity and meaning of the Bible, by suggesting that tradition was necessary for its interpretation. He was aware that many of Walton's precursors had been Catholics, and that elements of Walton's case rested on suggestions made by contemporary Jewish writers. Using arguments drawn in part from Buxtorf (catalogue no. 74), he defended the integrity of the Hebrew and Greek texts of the Old and New Testaments, and asserted the antiquity of the Hebrew vowel points. Nevertheless, as Owen's attacks on Socinian authors demonstrated, his work tried to establish sound principles for biblical interpretation, not to assert a simplistic reading of the text. It demonstrated the vitality and complexity of the literalist tradition among seventeenth-century Protestants, and the absence of any scholarly consensus for replacing it.

Peter Toon, *God's Statesman: The Life and Work of John Owen* (Exeter, 1971), p. 59; Donald K. McKim, 'John Owen's Doctrine of Scripture in Historical Perspective', *Evangelical Quarterly*, vol. 45 (1973), pp. 195-207; Carl Trueman, 'Faith Seeking Understanding: Some Neglected Aspects of John Owen's Understanding of Scriptural Interpretation', in A. N. S. Lane (ed.), *Interpreting the Bible: Historical and Theological Studies in Honour of David F. Wright* (Leicester, 1997), pp. 147-62.

77. Brian Walton
The Considerator Considered
London, 1659
8°: A⁴ B-T⁸ V⁴
122 × 74 mm
8° K 20 Th.

The reply which Walton composed to Owen's criticism of the Polyglot Bible was both scholarly and polemical. At the level of scholarship, Walton asserted that he was not following Catholic or Jewish teaching, but seeking to discover the true meaning of scripture, which he valued as highly as Owen. He suggested that the best way to establish the Bible's authority was to gain access to the original text, and that this could only be done through comparative work such as the London Polyglot. Unlike Owen, Walton praised the Authorized Version, pointing out that all translations contained acts of interpretation. He

Figure 66
Engraved portrait of Brian Walton, from the first volume of the London Polyglot Bible. Walton is shown at work, with the sources of the Polyglot and several other major works of continental scholarship behind him.
Catalogue no. 73, frontispiece.

was scathing about the effect which religious independents like Owen had had on the ecclesiastical order of England during the Civil Wars and Interregnum of the 1640s and 1650s. He argued that his scholarly work was written in Latin, but that, by replying to it in English, Owen was allowing his own doubts to reach the common people. He asserted that teaching like Owen's was responsible for a blind faith in the right of individuals to interpret the literal meaning of the Bible for themselves which had, in turn, helped to undermine the authority of the established Church and promote the growth of heretical sects in England.

This polemic was intended to marginalize Owen in the debate, by associating his fears with the excesses of the unlearned. Nevertheless, Walton's response also underlined his own belief in the authority of scripture to determine the teaching of the Church, and his conviction that the literal sense was the best way of understanding the text of the Bible, once that had been established correctly. For scholars like Walton and Owen, there was ultimately no alternative to a literal exegesis of scripture, even if they were willing to quarrel over the identity of the biblical text itself.

This copy of Walton's reply to Owen belonged to Thomas Hyde, a young orientalist who had assisted Walton with the Persian and Syriac sections of the Polyglot, and who eventually became Bodley's librarian.

78. Christian Ravis
A Discourse of the Oriental Tongues
London, 1648
12°: A⁴ B-E¹²
120 × 68 mm
8° R 34 Art. Seld.

Christian Ravis (1613–77) was a German orientalist from Berlin who was patronized from 1639 by James Ussher, archbishop of Armagh, in order to enable him to make a journey to the east to collect manuscripts. Ussher's funds were forwarded to Ravis by Samuel Hartlib. Ravis spent some time in Smyrna and Constantinople, assembling manuscripts on his own account, and returned to England in 1641 with his amanuensis, Nicolaus Petri. Ravis then lived in London for a time, depending on the charity of Ussher and of John Selden, but soon left to search for employment in the Netherlands. In Amsterdam in the mid-1640s, he met Hartlib's friend and collaborator, John Pell, and provided him with an Arabic manuscript of Apollonius's *Conics*, part of which Pell translated into Latin.

By the summer of 1647, Ravis had returned to England, where Hartlib was seeking to promote the teaching of oriental languages in London, as part of his plans to reform education in the capital and to provide its citizens with the proper means to interpret the Bible for themselves. Both Hartlib and Dury also canvassed the idea of employing Ravis as an intermediary to the Jews at this time, as well as using him as a source of information on eastern nations. In 1648, Ravis gave lectures on oriental languages which were sponsored by the London Presbyterian clergy of Sion College, and took place near St Paul's. Despite this support and attempts to petition Parliament on his behalf, Ravis was unable to establish himself in London, and instead sought a position at Oxford. He was briefly lecturer in Hebrew at Magdalen College, before setting off to try his luck at the University of Uppsala in Sweden, where, however, he soon found himself short of money once again. Throughout his career, Ravis discovered that circumstances conspired against him, but he also proved that his most notable characteristics were untrustworthiness and vain self-promotion.

Despite his unpleasant character, Ravis had figured significantly in the hopes and plans of English orientalists in the 1640s. He played on their expectations by proposing schemes whereby the teaching of eastern languages might assist in the conversion of the Jews, or the printing of the Koran might lead to its more effective refutation and the success of a mission to the Turks. He also possessed a number of important Arabic manuscripts, and could argue that the application of his skill in Hebrew to the interpretation of difficult places in the Bible might lead to the production of a better English translation. Ravis set out his theory of the relationships between the various oriental languages in his *Discourse*. This stressed the unity of the Semitic languages, and was intended as a preface to the grammar which he composed for them. According to Ravis, Hebrew was the oldest tongue, which had been corrupted at Babel into many different pronunciations, from which the modern Semitic languages resulted. Like many of his contemporaries, Ravis stressed the primitive copiousness of biblical Hebrew, in which a relatively restricted number of roots could express the whole of language. He argued that a general knowledge of oriental languages would aid in the comprehension and correction of the English Bible, and that people could easily be taught to read the Hebrew and English scriptures side by side. Ravis's *Discourse* thus justified his activities in London as a Hebrew lecturer, as well as advertising his skills to a broader public.

G. J. Toomer, *Eastern Wisdome and Learning: The Study of Arabic in Seventeenth-Century England* (Oxford, 1996), pp. 83-4, 142-5, 151-2 & 183-200; Anthony Wood, *Athenae Oxonienses* (new edition, edited by Philip Bliss, 4 vols, London, 1813-20), vol. 3, pp. 1130-33; Christian Ravis, *Christiani Ravii Berlinatis sesqi-decuria epistolarum adoptivarum* (London, 1648); Richard Parr (ed.), *The Life of the Most Reverend Father in God, James Usher* (London, 1686), pp. 623-4; *Hartlib Papers*, 3/3/32A-33B, 10/8/1A-2B, 15/6/27A-28B, 28/1/35A, 31/22/39B, 39/2/149A-B, 47/12/1A-B, 56/1/134A-B.

79. Arnold Boate
De textus hebraici veteris testamenti certitudine
Paris, 1650
4°: A-M⁴
163 × 101 mm
4° I 19 Th. Seld.

Arnold Boate (1600?-1653), who had served as a physician in Ireland, was another orientalist who received Ussher's patronage and who was friendly with Hartlib. Resident in Paris during the late 1640s and early 1650s, he reported to Hartlib about natural philosophical developments in the city, and kept Ussher informed about oriental books and manuscripts, and about the progress of French scholarship and theological debate. He was hopeful that the rise of Jansenism might encourage French Catholics to move towards Protestant doctrinal positions, but, at the same time, he was worried about the implications for Protestant theology of contemporary developments in both Catholic and Huguenot biblical criticism.

At the end of the 1630s, Boate had assisted a group of Ussher's protégés who were working on Aramiac, Greek and Syriac biblical materials. In Paris, he became increasingly suspicious about the uses to which such philological and comparative research could be put. His concerns were aroused by the continuing work of the Oratorian critic, Jean Morin, on the antiquity of the Samaritan Pentateuch (with Ussher's disciple, Francis Taylor, Boate had already attacked Morin's writings on the Septuagint in 1636), and by the observations of Louis Cappel, professor of Hebrew at the Protestant Academy of Saumur, on variant readings in the Old Testament. Boate felt that, in the hands of Morin and Cappel, oriental scholarship was being used to undermine the antiquity and authority of the Hebrew text of the Bible. He was particularly disturbed by Cappel's *Critica sacra* (Paris, 1650), which raised questions about the age of the vowel points in the Hebrew Bible, among other things, and denied that the surviving Hebrew text preserved the autographs of scripture.

The publication of Cappel's work (which had been completed by 1636) had been eagerly anticipated by scholars across Europe (Hartlib called it 'a great booke' as early as 1642; *Hartlib Papers*, 30/4/84A [*Ephemerides*]). It was delayed by worries, which Boate soon came to share, about the orthodoxy of its conclusions and only the intervention of Morin and other French Catholic divines ensured its eventual appearance. In 1650, Boate was active in encouraging Ussher to repudiate Cappel's work and in prodding Johannes Buxtorf the younger (see catalogue no. 74) to attack it. He also helped to persuade French Hebraists, at the Collège Royal in Paris and at universities in the provinces, to side with Buxtorf.

Boate's own work on the certainty and authority of the Hebrew text of the Old Testament, which was transmitted to Ussher via Hartlib, argued that Cappel had searched for and applied variant readings indiscriminately, even on occasion making them up. He proposed that Cappel was willing to trust the text of any version of the Old Testament in preference to that of the Hebrew, and that he had not taken account of the possibility that ancient translations of the Bible might have been made from corrupt copies. These did not necessarily represent the real tradition of the text, now accessible to scholars in numerous manuscripts. Boate preferred to trust the opinons of the Fathers, notably Augustine and Jerome, on the authenticity of the text rather than accept Cappel's conclusions. Boate's arguments generated a succession of replies from Cappel, and also correspondence between Cappel and Ussher, who was himself eventually tempted into print against the *Critica sacra*. Despite Ussher's support for the London Polyglot (catalogue no. 73), Boate considered that Walton's work would simply perpetuate Cappel's errors, and was worried that it would not improve on the printing and editing standards of the Paris Polyglot.

Although Boate's natural philosophy (see catalogue no. 63) was anti-Aristotelian, his approach to biblical criticism was in many ways sympathetic to that of the mainstream of contemporary Protestant neo-scholasticism. For those who believed that true Christian doctrine was founded exclusively on the literal interpretation of God's word in the Bible, it seemed increasingly necessary to defend the antiquity and authenticity of the Hebrew and Greek versions which made up the received text of scripture. Calvinists like Boate and Ussher (and, indeed, Hartlib and Dury) were eager to acquire new knowledge about the text and history of the Bible, but they were also concerned to shape its application in order not to threaten the literal sense or authority of scripture.

This copy of Boate's *De textus hebraici veteris testamenti certitudine* belonged to John Selden and bears his motto (see catalogue no. 74).

François Laplanche, *L'écriture, le sacré et l'histoire: Érudits et politiques protestants devant la Bible en France au XVIIe siècle* (Amsterdam, 1986), pp. 181–327, especially 300–1; Georg Schnedermann, *Die Controverse des Ludovicus Cappellus mit den Buxtorfen über das Alter der Hebräischen Punctation* (Leipzig, 1879); Richard A. Muller, 'The Debate over the Vowel Points and the Crisis in Orthodox Hermeneutics', *Journal of Medieval and Renaissance Studies*, vol. 10 (1980), pp. 53–72; Paul Auvray, 'Jean Morin (1591–1659)', *Révue Biblique*, vol. 66 (1959), pp. 397–414; J. C. H. Lebram, 'Ein Streit um die Hebräische Bibel und die Septuaginta', in Th. H. Lunsingh Scheurleer and G. H. M. Posthumus Meyjes (eds.), *Leiden University in the Seventeenth Century* (Leiden, 1975), pp. 20–63; James Ussher and William Eyre, *De textus hebraici veteris testamenti variantibus lectionibus ad Ludovicum Cappelum epistola* (London, 1652); Richard Parr (ed.), *The Life of the Most Reverend Father in God, James Usher* (London, 1686), pp. 491, 498–9, 533–5, 557–60, 562, 564–6, 568–79, 583–9, 605–6 & 620–2; Bodleian Library, Ms. Selden supra 108, fols. 80 & 86 (Letters of Taylor and Boate); *Hartlib Papers*, 28/1/47B, 28/2/16B, 28/2/29B–30A, 30/4/84A, 36/1/17A–20B, 39/1/6A–7B.

80. Portrait of James Ussher
    By William Fletcher
    Oil on canvas
    910 × 760 mm
    Lane Poole no. 125

Ussher is represented by catalogue no. 81.

R. Lane Poole, *Catalogue of Portraits in the Possession of the University, Colleges, City, and County of Oxford* (3 vols, Oxford, 1912–26), vol. 1, p. 51.

Figure 67
Portrait of James Ussher, archbishop of Armagh and primate of all Ireland. Ussher's lasting fame was ensured by his dating of the start of the creation of the world to the evening before the 23rd October, 4004 B.C. Catalogue no. 80.

81. **James Ussher**
   The Annals of the World
   London, 1658
   fol. in 4s: A⁶ B–6F⁴
   260 × 175 mm
   Vet. A3 c. 95

James Ussher (1581–1656), archbishop of Armagh, was the pre-eminent figure in the contemporary Church of Ireland, and a leading patron of scholarship at Trinity College, Dublin. A staunch defender of episcopacy, he was nevertheless respected on all sides during the religious upheavals of the 1640s and 1650s, and regarded as the person most likely to achieve an accommodation between the Presbyterians and the Church of England. As such, he was valued by Hartlib and Dury, both of whom helped him at times with his scholarly work and looked to him as a potential patron for their own schemes.

Despite his success as a churchman, Ussher is perhaps most famous for having dated the start of the creation to the evening before 23rd October, 4004 B.C. Ussher calculated this timing in his *Annals*, a work of biblical chronology which he published in Latin in 1650 (Hartlib noted its progress through the press with great interest), and which was translated into English in 1658. The book was the fruit of many years labour; as early as the summer of 1640, Ussher had been reported 'spend[ing] constantly all the afternoones' in the Bodleian working at it (Constantine Adams to Hartlib, *Hartlib Papers*, 15/8/3A-4B).

In the *Annals*, Ussher developed the chronological work of many earlier scholars, in particular Joseph Justus Scaliger (who had pioneered the use of the Julian period in calendrical calculations) to provide a framework for dating the whole Bible historically. He argued that, although scripture itself only tended to take notice of entire years, the Holy Ghost had left clues in the Bible which allowed the critic to establish a precise chronology of its events, through the application to the text of the results of astronomical calculations and its comparison with the dates of pagan history. Ussher's system had the advantage of preserving several attractive numerical symmetries, for example the ancient Jewish notion, adopted by Christians, that the creation anticipated the birth of the Messiah by 4,000 years, but it was also heavily dependent on classical chronologies and on an interpretation of the calendar which already seemed out-dated to many scholars.

Although not wholly original, Ussher's work was nevertheless influential and became widely accepted, not least because its dates were later incorporated into the margins of some editions of the Authorized Version. However, Ussher's chronology rested too heavily on the Hebrew text of Old Testament to escape controversy even in his own day. Its findings were attacked by those who were persuaded that the Greek translation of the Old Testament (the Septuagint) or the Samaritan Pentateuch (both of which presented different chronologies from the Hebrew) were more reliable witnesses to the dictation of the Holy Ghost, or that they concurred more closely with the evidence of astronomy and pagan history. Yet, in the opinion of Hartlib, and perhaps of many others, Ussher's critics were churlish individuals who were unwilling to admit their own debts to his scholarship. Despite such debates, most seventeenth-century readers of the Bible would have agreed with Ussher that it ought, in principle, to have been possible to establish an accurate and detailed biblical chronology.

Illustrated opposite is the title-page from the *Annals*, engraved by Francis Barlow and Richard Gaywood. This shows a number of the crucial figures and episodes from Ussher's chronology. Adam and Eve are flanked by the figures of Solomon and Nebuchadnezzar, the builder and destroyer of the first Temple, which is also shown both in its glory and after its fall. The engraving also depicts the second Temple, built after Cyrus allowed the return of the Jews to Jerusalem, and its eventual destruction. The figures of Cyrus and of Vespasian (who was Emperor at the time of the destruction of Herod's Temple,

Biblical Criticism

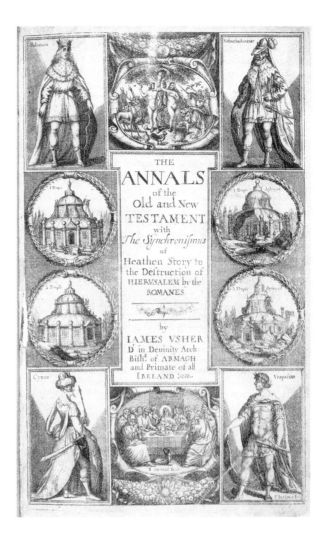

Figure 68

The title-page of Ussher's *Annals of the World*, illustrating, in synchrony, scenes from the Old and New Testament. Depicted are, from top to bottom: Adam and Eve in the Garden of Eden, flanked by the figures of Solomon and Nebuchadnezzar (builder and destroyer of the first Temple respectively); the first Temple and its destruction; the second Temple and its destruction; and, flanking a scene of the Last Supper, the figures of Cyrus and Vespasian (facilitator and destroyer of the second Temple respectively). From catalogue no. 82.

in A. D. 70) flank a depiction of the Last Supper. This copy of the *Annals* has also been extra-illustrated by the pasting in of a contemporary engraved portrait of Ussher, which shows him holding 'God's Word', the Bible, in his hand. It was executed for the London printseller, Peter Stent, who advertised it for sale in 1653, 1658, 1662, and 1663.

R. Buick Knox, *James Ussher, Archbishop of Armagh* (Cardiff, 1967); Hugh Trevor-Roper, *Catholics, Anglicans and Puritans* (London, 1987), pp. 120-65; James Barr, 'Why the World was Created in 4004 B.C.: Archbishop Ussher and Biblical Chronology', *Bulletin of the John Rylands University Library of Manchester*, vol. 67 (1984-85), pp. 575-608; Alexander Globe, *Peter Stent, London Printseller, circa 1642–1665* (Vancouver, 1985), p. 85, no. 291; *Hartlib Papers*, 15/8/3A-4B, 28/1/52A, 28/2/51B, 29/2/53A-54B, 29/5/24A, 29/5/37A, 31/22/9B, 31/22/24B-25A, 47/9/16A-17B.

Biblical Criticism

82. Portrait of Samuel Bochart
    By P. du Bosc
    Oil on canvas
    760 × 630 mm
    Lane Poole no. 132

    Illustrated on p. 91. Bochart is represented by catalogue nos. 35 and 83.

    R. Lane Poole, *Catalogue of Portraits in the Possession of the University, Colleges, City, and County of Oxford* (3 vols, Oxford, 1912–26), vol. 1, pp. 53–54.

83. Samuel Bochart
    Geographiae sacrae pars prior
    Caen, 1646
    fol. in 4s: â⁴ ê⁴ î⁴ ô² A-5X⁴ *-4*⁴ 5*⁶
    268 × 145 mm
    Douce B subt. 151 (1)

Phaleg, the first part of *Geographia sacra* by Samuel Bochart, traced the dispersion of peoples following the confusion of languages at the Tower of Babel. The various locations into which the different nations descended from the sons of Noah moved are shown on the map, engraved by R. Hubert, illustrated opposite. From the near East, people eventually spread to inhabit the entire globe.

Bochart's history of nations and languages was widely known in the late seventeenth century, and provided the inspiration for many similar works by other authors. It was a notable attempt to construct a single historical narrative from the available Semitic and classical sources, which, like others of its kind, tended at times to accept interpolated or forged material at face value. *Phaleg* began from the premise that the account of the settlement of the world given in chapter 10 of Genesis was an accurate one. The evidence for this could be deduced from a study of pagan religions, which demonstrated that Noah (or a figure who could be identified as Noah) was worshipped as a common ancestor in all ancient traditions. The work continued with an account of the history of the Flood, explaining that paradise, and the first human settlement, had been in Babylonia; that the Ark had come to rest on the highest peaks of Assyria, the Gordiaei, which were to the east of the Taurus mountains; and that the original language, Hebrew, had decayed in various ways since the time of the dispersion of peoples. It continued with the story of the travels of each of Noah's three sons and their first descendants.

Biblical Criticism

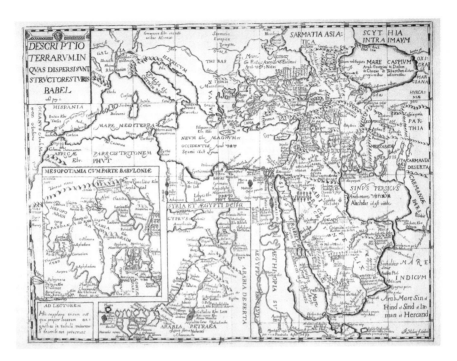

Figure 69
Samuel Bochart's map of the various locations into which the different nations descended from the sons of Noah migrated after the dispersion of peoples. From catalogue no. 83.

Bochart's account of the history of language postulated that the primitive Hebrew had been communicated to the Canaanites, and by them to the Phoenicians. In *Chanaan*, the second, larger part of *Geographia sacra*, Bochart was principally concerned with the language, voyages, and colonies of the Phoenicians. Here, he argued that the settlement and original language of the British Isles derived from Phoenician mariners, who had come there in search of tin. Although Bochart's work gave primacy to the historical narrative of the Bible, and to the antiquity of the primitive Hebrew language, it did not always defer to the dates mentioned in the Old Testament. Instead, Bochart often preferred to rely on the chronology of the Samaritan Pentateuch. Such choices reflected his humanist concern with the reconstruction of the most ancient sources for his work and his conviction that language and custom were subject to providential and historical change.

Edward Herbert Smith, *Samuel Bochart* (Caen, 1833); François Laplanche, *L'écriture, le sacré et l'histoire: Érudits et politiques protestants devant la Bible en France au XVIIe siècle* (Amsterdam, 1986), pp. 250–4; A. Dupront, *Pierre-Daniel Huet et l'exégèse comparatiste au XVIIe siècle* (Paris, 1930), pp. 95–9; Biblioteca Medicea Laurenziana, Florence, Ms. Ashburnham 1866, numbers 64–69 (Correspondence of Bochart and Huet concerning *Phaleg*).

84. Isaac La Peyrère
Men Before Adam
London, 1655-56
8°: A-2E⁸
134 × 76 mm
Wood 889(3)

Born at Bordeaux into a French Protestant family, which may perhaps have had Jewish ancestry, Isaac La Peyrère (1596–1676) was the author of one of the most controversial books of the seventeenth century. According to La Peyrère, Adam and Eve had been created to be the parents of the Jews, God's chosen people. At the time of their creation, the Gentiles already existed, and peopled the whole earth outside Eden; at the Fall, Adam's sin was imputed back to them. Many of the events related in the Old Testament affected the Jews only, for example, Noah's Flood was confined to Palestine.

La Peyrère had originally developed his ideas about the pre-Adamites in the context of a new theory of Jewish Messianism which he first advanced in the early 1640s, when he was working as a secretary to the Prince de Condé. He argued that it was necessary for Christians to purify and simplify their religion in order to attract the Jews to join it, and that a messianic ruler (possibly Condé himself) would emerge to restore the Jews and establish a universal monarchy. The Jews remained God's original, chosen people; they were the descendants of Adam and it was wrong to persecute or vilify them. Their salvation was an essential prelude to universal redemption.

La Peyrère was discouraged from publishing his pre-Adamite theory in the book which he produced in 1643, *Du rappel des Juifs*, but he continued to develop it during the ensuing decade. Travels which he undertook in Scandinavia alerted him to the problem of the ancestry of both the native inhabitants of North America and the eskimos of Greenland. Neither of these peoples seemed to fit easily into the genealogies set out in the book of Genesis, thus giving support to the hypothesis that the biblical account of the dispersion of peoples related to the Jews alone. With the encouragement of the exiled Queen Christina of Sweden, La Peyrère was eventually persuaded to publish his pre-Adamite theory in Holland in 1655. Condemnations swiftly followed, leading to La Peyrère's arrest and imprisonment in Brussels. Shortly afterwards, he converted to Catholicism and was taken to Rome, where he had an audience with Pope Alexander VII, and abjured his heresies.

The newly-penitent La Peyrère deployed the hypothesis of men before Adam in order to attack the Calvinist method of interpreting scripture according to the literal sense, reason, and the individual conscience. He argued that this method had led him into his heresy, and that belief in pre-Adamites was indeed consistent with a Calvinist approach to the Bible. Catholics, in contrast, were bound to accept the ruling of the Church on disputed issues, and to interpret scripture in accordance with its teaching. As a result, following his conversion, La Peyrère repudiated his former views because he was instructed to do so by the Pope. He continued, however, to hope for the establishment of a universal, Christian monarchy, perhaps under the Pope's direction. The messianic and pre-Adamite themes of La Peyrère's early work continued to appear in his later writings, and were the subject of discussions with the young Richard Simon in the 1670s, after La Peyrère had become a lay member of an Oratorian seminary near Paris. Simon, who later became one of the greatest of contemporary linguists and biblical critics, and whose own work on the inconsistencies in Protestant approaches to scripture proved deeply influential, was unimpressed with La Peyrère's learning, although no doubt taken with his skill in sceptical argument and confessional polemic.

La Peyrère's *Prae-Adamitae* was translated into English almost immediately after its initial publication in Holland. In August 1655, Hartlib noted proudly that he had discovered the identity of the author of *Prae-Adamitae*, 'as I take it le Pere ... or Liperira a french-man' (*Hartlib Papers*, 29/5/42A [*Ephemerides*, 1655]). On 24th October, the stationers Thomas Underhill and Nathaniel Webb petitioned for the suppression of the English translation which was then being printed by Francis Leach, on the grounds that the book was 'putting a blasphemous slur on the Bible testimony concerning the creation of man' (*Calendar of State Papers Domestic*, 1655, p. 393).

Many contemporary Protestants were worried by the implications of La Peyrère's work, and by the doubts which it cast on the historical narrative of the Bible. Mainstream English churchmen and Calvinists were especially worried about the effect *Men Before Adam* might have in a country where the teachings of several new sects, notably the Quakers, already threatened the traditional authority of scripture. In some ways, it was the timing of the publication of La Peyrère's ideas, rather than the ideas themselves, which generated anxiety. As Simon later remarked, La Peyrère was not an original or a consistent scholar. His work contained several familiar libertine ideas and criticisms of traditional exegesis, often founded on well-known classical or Jewish precedents. The notion that there might have been some kind of people before Adam had already been explored, for example by Paracelsus, as a solution to the problem of the settlement of the Americas (for more orthodox answers to this, see catalogue nos. 49 and 50). Sir Thomas Browne (see catalogue no. 47) had rejected Paracelsus's 'non-Adamical men' (*Pseudodoxia epidemica*, Book 4, chapter 11), but more radical contemporaries were also aware of the textual ambiguities in

Genesis to which La Peyrère would later draw attention. Thus, writing of his career as a Ranter in the later 1640s, Laurence Clarkson remarked that 'I neither believed that *Adam* was the first Creature, but that there was a Creation before him, which world I thought was eternal' (*The Lost Sheep Found*, in Smith (ed.), p. 185). As Browne had outlined in *Religio medici* (1642-43), there were perfectly good orthodox reponses to such beliefs, and the doubts which spawned them. It was quite possible to accept the literal truth of scripture without demanding that the Bible explain itself at every turn, for example by accounting for the peopling of the cities which Cain built after the murder of Abel (Genesis 4). The solution to the problems raised by La Peyrère which most English Protestants adopted was to urge a greater concentration on what the text of the Bible actually said, rather than worrying about what it did not say. This was accompanied by a widespread rejection of the notion of personal inspiration espoused by Clarkson or the Quakers, and the renewed advocacy instead of the close reading of scripture, especially under the guidance of an educated clergy, as the safe route to religious understanding.

Richard H. Popkin, *Isaac La Peyrère (1596-1676)* (Leiden, 1987), especially pp. 5-41; Susanna Åkerman, *Queen Christina of Sweden and her Circle* (Leiden, 1991), pp. 202-7; René Pintard, *Le libertinage érudit* (2 vols, Paris, 1943), vol. 1, pp. 358-62 & 420-4; Giuliano Gliozzi, *Adamo e il Nuovo Mondo* (Florence, 1977), pp. 514-94; Isaac La Peyrère, *Lettre de la Peyrere a Philoteme* (Paris, 1658); Richard Simon, *Lettres choisies* (new edition, edited by M. Bruzen la Martinière, 4 vols, Amsterdam, 1730), vol. 2, pp. 1-26 and vol. 3, pp. 41-51; *Calendar of State Papers Domestic* (1655), p. 393; Nigel Smith (ed.), *A Collection of Ranter Writings from the 17th Century* (London, 1983); Sir Thomas Browne, *Religio medici*, in *Selected Writings*, edited by Geoffrey Keynes (London, 1968), p. 29; *Hartlib Papers*, 29/5/42A.

85. Georg Horn
Arca Noae sive historia imperiorum et regnorum
Leiden, 1666
12°: *^{12} 2*^{4} A-2A^{12} 2B^{8}
102 × 50 mm
8° R 23 Art. BS.

Georg Horn (1620-70), professor of history at Leiden, was a frequent correspondent of Hartlib on subjects ranging from alchemy to universal history (to which genre Horn was himself a notable contributor). He was a supporter of the English Presbyterians, and a proponent of a militant union of Protestants to oppose the power of the Papacy. During the early 1650s, he discussed the

Biblical Criticism

Figure 70

The title-page from Georg Horn's *Arca Noae* showing the Ark tossing on stormy seas.
A lion, a bear, a winged leopard and an eagle fight for dominion over a terrestrial globe in the skies above the Ark. They represent the four great empires that will rule the earth before the coming of the kingdom of the saints.
From catalogue no. 85.

problem of teaching biblical history with Hartlib, exploring the possibility of presenting his findings in tabular and pictorial form. He also expressed his support for the short chronology of the Hebrew Bible, in preference to the longer history given by the dates in the Septuagint.

Horn's writings were concerned with the defence of orthodox biblical history and were successful in accommodating fresh materials to traditional chronology. In 1652, Horn had tackled the problem of the population of the Americas, arguing that there had not been enough people before the Flood to inhabit the whole world. America had therefore been settled after the Flood, probably by Phoenician navigators, Scythian and Tartar (and thus, possibly, Jewish) migrants, and Chinese sailors. Later, Horn turned his attention to the differences between biblical, classical, and oriental chronologies. The motivation for this came largely from the Jesuit discovery of the antiquity of Chinese history, which seemed to some to provide a continuous record older than that given by scripture. (On this basis, John Webb, see catalogue no. 73, argued that Chinese had been the primitive language used by Noah.) Horn was willing to identify figures from biblical history with the earliest characters mentioned in the Chinese annals, and, indeed, to suggest that China had initially been peopled with the offspring of the banished Cain, but he rejected the suggestion that Chinese records antedated the Flood. He advanced a traditional account of the dispersion of peoples, following Genesis chapters 10 and 11, and argued, for example, that the Gauls and Britons were descended from Japhet's son, Javan, via his son Dodanim, and that the Germans were the descandants of Gomer, via Ashkenaz.

Well aware of the extent of contemporary European power and expansion, Horn wished to interpret as fulfilled the prophecy given in Genesis 9: 27 (which suggested that Japhet's descendants would come to rule the whole world). Horn's work thus reinforced the standard ethnographic opinions of his contemporaries. It concluded that neither the discovery of new peoples nor the disclosure of new records constituted a sufficient reason to modify the accepted historical narrative derived from scripture.

The elaborate title-page of *Arca Noae* was engraved by Wingandorp and shows the Ark tossed on stormy seas. Four animals – a lion, a bear, a winged leopard and an eagle – fight for dominion over the globe in the skies above the Ark. These presumably represent the four beasts of Daniel's vision (Daniel 7), modified by the inclusion of the Imperial Habsburg eagle (perhaps justified by the apocalyptic vision of an eagle in 2 Esdras 11-12). They symbolize the four great empires which will rule the world in succession before the eventual coming of the kingdom of the saints. The engraving places *Arca Noae* in the apocalyptic context which, according to Horn, dominated human history and reinforces the book's description of the division of the world into kingdoms and empires. Providence had ordered the growth and decline of nations. It would, in due course, bring about the downfall of contemporary tyranny (for Horn, the papacy and its allies) and the establishment of millenarian harmony on earth.

D. Nauta, 'Georgius Hornius', in D. Nauta *et al.* (eds.), *Biografisch Lexicon voor de Geschiedenis van het Nederlandse Protestantisme* (3 vols, Kampen, 1978-88), vol. 2, pp. 261-3; Arno Borst, *Der Turmbau von Babel* (4 vols. in 6 parts, Stuttgart, 1957-63, reprinted Munich, 1995), vol. 3, part 1, pp. 1305-7; J. C. H. Lebram, 'Ein Streit um die Hebraïsche Bibel und die Septuaginta', in Th. H. Lunsingh Scheurleer and G. H. M. Posthumus Meyjes (eds.), *Leiden University in the Seventeenth Century* (Leiden, 1975), pp. 20-63; Georg Horn, *De originibus americanis libri quatuor* (The Hague, 1652); John Webb, *An Historical Essay Endeavouring a Probability that the Language of the Empire of China is the Primitive Language* (London, 1669); *Hartlib Papers*, 4/3/121A-B, 16/2/1A-36B, 60/7/1A-6B.

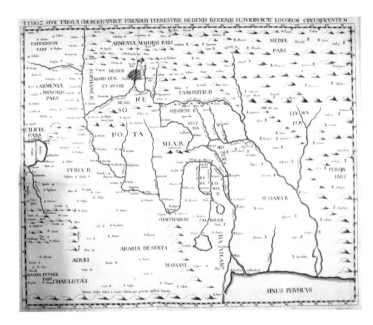

Figure 71
Marmaduke Carver's map of the location of the Garden of Eden. Carver located paradise not in Mesopotamia as many commentators had done, but in Armenia, close to the site of the landing of the Ark, which he identified with Mount Gordiaeus. From catalogue no. 86.

86. Marmaduke Carver
A Discourse of the Terrestrial Paradise
London, 1666
8°: A⁸ a⁸ B–L⁸ M⁴
135 × 73 mm
8° R 71(3) Med.

Carver's work, which was originally composed in about 1640, took issue with the accepted view (as expressed in the work of Franciscus Junius, and followed by Ralegh and others) that paradise had been situated in Mesopotamia. Arguing in part from the works of ancient geographers, Carver suggested instead that the literal sense of the Bible was served better by assuming that Eden had been placed at the sources of the rivers mentioned in Genesis 2. He therefore located paradise in Armenia, close to the landing place of the Ark, which (like Bochart, catalogue no. 83) he identified with Mount Gordiaeus. He hoped that his solution to the geographical problems of Genesis would aid the Christian reader in 'believing the infallible Veracity of the Holy Scriptures' (sig. a6 verso), and combat the blasphemous doubts of the Ranters and Quakers. Although he was less willing than some to rely on the findings of modern geographers and travellers, Carver was optimistic that the investigation of nature would produce information which complemented the narrative of the Bible and which gave support to orthodox techniques of interpretation.

An electronic index and full-text search facility may be found
in the electronic edition of this catalogue at http://www.mhs.ox.ac.uk/